Copyright © 2025 by Riley Victor

All rights reserved. No part of this book may be reproduced, stored in a retrieval system, or transmitted in any form or by any means, electronic, mechanical, photocopying, recording, or otherwise, without prior written permission by the author.

i

This thoughtfully created guide is dedicated to Microsoft Word, offering a comprehensive, step-by-step exploration of its versatile features and powerful tools. From mastering the basics to unlocking advanced techniques, it's designed to help you build practical skills and enhance your confidence in creating and managing professional-quality documents.

Whether you're a student, a curious learner, a complete beginner, or a seasoned professional, this book is tailored to meet your needs. Let it inspire your creativity, refine your document design abilities, and empower you on your journey to mastering Microsoft Word.

Table of Content

Part 1: Getting Started

Chapter 1: Introduction

Microsoft Word is a powerful word-processing application developed by Microsoft. It's part of the Microsoft Office Suite and is designed to help users create, edit, format, and share documents effortlessly. Whether you're drafting a simple letter, creating a professional report, or designing a visually appealing flyer, Microsoft Word offers the tools and features you need.

Key Features of Microsoft Word:

- User-Friendly Interface: A clean, intuitive layout that makes it easy for beginners to navigate.
- Formatting Tools: From fonts and colors to page layouts and styles, you can create visually stunning documents.
- Collaboration Capabilities: Share documents, track changes, and work with others in real-time.
- Templates: Ready-made designs for resumes, reports, newsletters, and more.

Think of Word as your digital typewriter with a supercharged toolbox to help you do more, faster.

Why Microsoft Word is Essential in Today's World

In a world increasingly reliant on digital communication, Microsoft Word is more than just a tool—it's a necessity. Here's why:

1. Universal Use:
   o Word documents are used across industries, from business and education to healthcare and government.
   o Employers often expect proficiency in Word as a basic computer skill.
2. Professional Presentation:
   o A well-formatted document can make a lasting impression, whether it's a resume, proposal, or report.
   o Word's tools help ensure your documents are polished and error-free.
3. Versatility and Integration:
   o Create diverse types of content, from simple letters to complex reports.
   o Integrates seamlessly with other Microsoft Office apps like Excel and PowerPoint.
4. Accessibility:
   o Available across multiple platforms: Windows, macOS, web, and mobile.
   o Cloud storage via OneDrive ensures you can access your work anywhere.

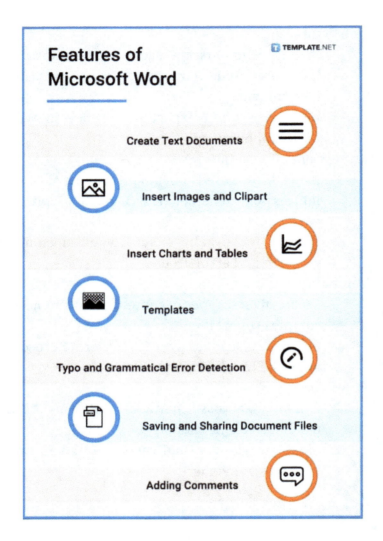

Overview of the Book's Approach

Learning a new tool like Microsoft Word can feel overwhelming at first, but this guide is designed to make the process simple, engaging, and effective. Here's how we'll help you master Word:

1. Step-by-Step Guidance:
   o Each chapter breaks down tasks into clear, manageable steps.
   o Visual aids like screenshots accompany explanations for added clarity.
2. Real-World Applications:
   o Examples and exercises focus on practical scenarios, like writing a resume, creating an event invitation, or preparing a meeting agenda.
3. Interactive Learning:
   o Chapters include hands-on practice exercises to reinforce your learning.
   o Tips and best practices are highlighted throughout to help you work smarter.
4. Encouraging Progress:
   o No prior experience? No problem! The book assumes no previous knowledge and builds your confidence as you progress.

A Personal Note from the Author

Learning Microsoft Word is like unlocking a door to endless possibilities. Whether you're starting a new career, going back to school, or simply exploring the world of digital documents, this guide is your trusted companion. Remember, every expert was once a beginner. Take it step by step, and before you know it, you'll be creating professional documents with ease.

Chapter 2: Setting Up Microsoft Word

G etting started with Microsoft Word begins with installing it on your device. Here's a step-by-step guide to help you through the process:

Choose Your Microsoft Office Plan

1. Visit the Official Microsoft Website:
   - o Navigate to https://www.microsoft.com.
   - o Look for the Microsoft Office or Microsoft 365 section.
2. Select a Plan:
   - o Microsoft 365 Subscription: Includes Word, Excel, PowerPoint, and other apps with cloud storage.
   - o One-Time Purchase: Ideal for those who need only Word and prefer a one-time payment.
3. Sign Up or Log In:
   - o Create a Microsoft account or sign in with your existing one to proceed.

Download and Install Word

1. Download the Installer:
   - o After purchasing, you'll receive a download link. Click it to download the setup file.
2. Run the Installer:

- Locate the downloaded file (usually in your "Downloads" folder) and double-click to run it.
3. Follow On-Screen Instructions:
   - Choose your preferred language and install location.
   - Wait for the installation to complete.

Activate Word

1. Open Microsoft Word:
   - Launch the app from your desktop or Start menu.
2. Sign In:
   - Use the same Microsoft account you used to purchase Word.
3. Enter Your Product Key (if applicable):
   - Enter the 25-character key provided during purchase.
4. Verify Activation:
   - Word will notify you once it's activated and ready to use.

Understanding Word Versions: Desktop, Web, and Mobile

Microsoft Word offers flexibility with different versions to suit your needs. Here's an overview of each:

1. Desktop Version:

- Platform: Windows and macOS.
- Features: Full-featured version with advanced tools for creating, editing, and formatting documents.

- Best For: Professionals, students, and anyone working extensively on documents.

2. Web Version:

- Platform: Accessible via any browser at https://office.com.
- Features: Basic tools for creating and editing documents. Cloud-based with automatic saving.
- Best For: Quick edits and collaboration on shared files.

3. Mobile Version:

- Platform: iOS and Android.
- Features: Optimized for small screens with essential features for editing on the go.
- Best For: Users needing access to Word while traveling.

Quick Comparison Table:

Feature	Desktop	Web	Mobile
Full Features	✔	✖	✖
Cloud Integration	✔	✔	✔
Offline Access	✔	✖	✔

System Requirements and Updates

Before installing Word, ensure your device meets the system requirements:

Minimum System Requirements:

1. Windows:

- ○ Operating System: Windows 10 or later.
- ○ Processor: 1.6 GHz or faster, 2-core.
- ○ Memory: 4 GB RAM (64-bit) or 2 GB RAM (32-bit).
- ○ Storage: 4 GB available disk space.
- ○ Display: 1280 x 768 screen resolution.
2. macOS:
   - ○ Operating System: macOS Mojave (10.14) or later.
   - ○ Processor: Intel or Apple Silicon.
   - ○ Memory: 4 GB RAM.
   - ○ Storage: 10 GB available disk space.
3. Mobile:
   - ○ iOS: Requires iOS 13.0 or later.
   - ○ Android: Requires Android 6.0 or later.

Updating Microsoft Word:

1. Enable Automatic Updates:
   - ○ Open Word, go to File > Account > Update Options, and select Enable Updates.
2. Check for Updates Manually:
   - ○ Go to File > Account > Update Options > Update Now.
3. Why Updates Matter:
   - ○ Ensure security patches are installed.
   - ○ Access new features and improved functionality.

With Word successfully installed, updated, and ready to go, you're all set to explore its interface and begin creating documents.

Chapter 3: Exploring the Interface

T he first step in your Microsoft Word journey is understanding its interface. Here's how to open Word and what to expect:

Launch Microsoft Word

1. Windows Users:
    - o Click the Start Menu and type "Word" in the search bar.
    - o Select Microsoft Word from the results.
2. macOS Users:
    - o Open the Applications folder and click Microsoft Word.
3. Mobile or Web Users:
    - o Launch the app from your mobile device or go to office.com.

Start a New Document

1. When Word opens, you'll see the Start Screen. Here, you can:
    - o Open recent files.
    - o Create a new document by clicking Blank Document.
    - o Use templates for specific types of documents (e.g., resumes or newsletters).
2. Once you select Blank Document, the main interface appears, ready for exploration.

Overview of the Ribbon and Tabs

The Ribbon is your main control center in Word, located at the top of the window. It's organized into Tabs that group related tools together.

Key Tabs and Their Functions:

1. Home Tab:
   - Tools for basic text formatting, such as font, size, color, and alignment.
   - Clipboard options like Cut, Copy, and Paste.
   - Paragraph settings (e.g., bullet points and spacing).
2. Insert Tab:
   - Add elements like tables, pictures, shapes, charts, headers, and footers.
   - Insert hyperlinks, text boxes, and WordArt.
3. Layout Tab:
   - Adjust page margins, orientation, size, and indentation.
   - Tools for columns, spacing, and alignment.
4. References Tab:
   - Add citations, bibliographies, captions, and footnotes.
   - Create a table of contents.
5. Review Tab:
   - Tools for proofreading, including spell check and word count.
   - Enable Track Changes for collaboration and use Comments for feedback.
6. View Tab:

- o Change the document view (e.g., Print Layout, Read Mode).
- o Access Zoom and navigation tools.

Tips for Navigating the Ribbon:

- Use the Search Bar (in newer Word versions) at the top of the window to find tools quickly.
- Double-click any tab to hide or show the Ribbon for a cleaner workspace.

The Quick Access Toolbar

The Quick Access Toolbar is a small customizable toolbar located at the top-left corner of the Word window. It provides shortcuts to frequently used commands.

Customizing the Quick Access Toolbar:

1. Click the Dropdown Arrow next to the toolbar.
2. Select or deselect commands (e.g., Save, Undo, Redo).
3. To add more options:
   - o Click More Commands.
   - o Choose tools from the list and click Add.

The Status Bar and Zoom Controls

At the bottom of the Word window, you'll find the Status Bar, which provides useful information about your document.

Key Elements of the Status Bar:

1. Page Count: Displays the current page and total pages (e.g., Page 1 of 3).
2. Word Count: Tracks the number of words in your document.
3. Language: Indicates the language settings for spell checking.
4. Track Changes: Shows if the feature is enabled.

Zoom Controls:

- Found on the right side of the Status Bar.
- Use the slider to zoom in or out, or click the +/- buttons for precise adjustments.

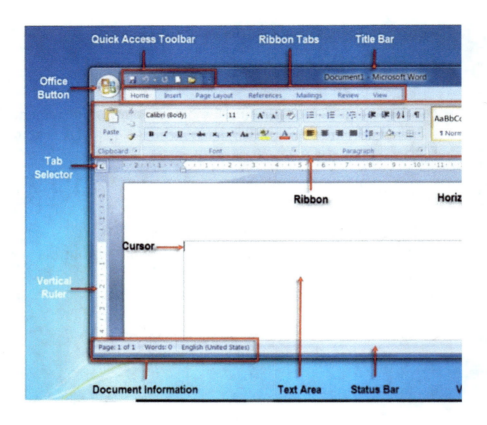

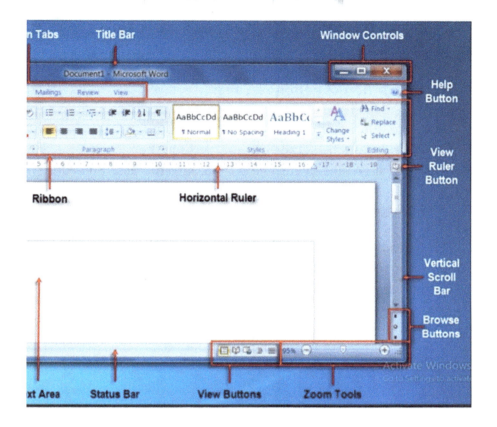

Customizing the Interface for Your Needs

Tailoring Word's interface ensures it works best for your preferences and tasks.

Change the Ribbon Display:

1. Click the small arrow in the top-right corner of the screen.
2. Choose from:
   - o Show Tabs Only for a cleaner look.

o Show Tabs and Commands for full access to the Ribbon.

Add or Remove Ribbon Tabs:

1. Go to File > Options > Customize Ribbon.
2. Check or uncheck tabs to show or hide them.
3. Rearrange tabs by dragging them into the desired order.

Change the Theme:

1. Go to File > Account > Office Theme.
2. Choose from options like Colorful, Dark Gray, or White to match your aesthetic.

Part 2: Creating and Managing Documents

Chapter 4: Starting a New Document

T he first step in working with Microsoft Word is opening a blank document, where you can start creating your content from scratch. Here's how you can do it:

Launching Word

1. Windows:
   - Click the Start Menu and type "Word," then select Microsoft Word from the search results.
2. macOS:
   - Open the Applications folder, find Microsoft Word, and click it.
3. Mobile/Tablet:
   - Tap the Microsoft Word app to open it.

Opening a Blank Document

1. When you first launch Microsoft Word, you'll see the Start Screen with different options.
2. Click Blank Document to start with a fresh page where you can begin typing your content.

Using Templates for Quick Setups

Microsoft Word offers a wide range of templates to help you get started quickly with specific types of documents, such as resumes, reports, newsletters, and more. Templates can save you time and effort in formatting.

Accessing Templates

1. From the Start Screen, under the New tab, you'll see a variety of templates categorized by document type (e.g., letters, resumes, brochures, etc.).

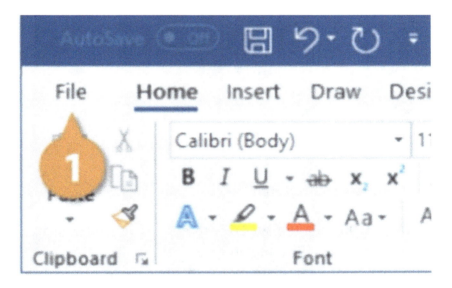

2. To access more templates, click on the Search for Online Templates box at the top of the page.

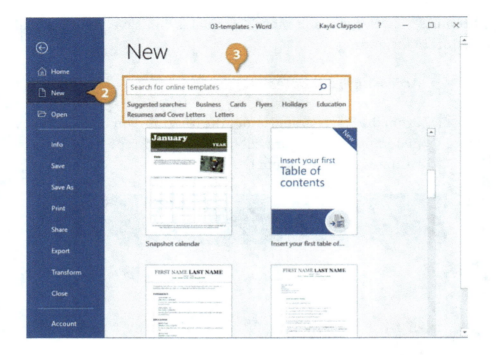

Choosing a Template

1. Scroll through the available templates or use the search bar to find a specific template (e.g., "resume").
2. Click on the template that suits your needs. A preview will appear, showing how the document looks.
3. Once you've chosen, click Create to open the template and begin customizing it.

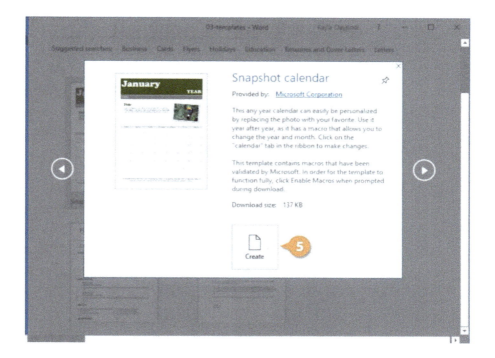

Customizing Your Template

1. Replace Text: Click on any placeholder text (e.g., "Your Name") to replace it with your own content.
2. Adjust Formatting: Change fonts, colors, and layout to personalize the template according to your preferences.

Tip: Templates are a great way to get started without worrying about formatting. However, you can always start fresh with a blank document and design it your way if you prefer.

Switching Between Documents

As you work in Microsoft Word, you may have multiple documents open at once. Switching between documents is a simple process that helps you stay organized and productive.

Using the Taskbar (Windows)

1. If you're using Windows, any open Word document will appear as an icon in the Taskbar (usually at the bottom of the screen).
2. To switch between documents, simply click on the Word icon in the Taskbar, and then click the document you want to open.

Using the Window Tab (macOS)

1. On a Mac, each document will be represented as a window in the Dock at the bottom of the screen.
2. Click the Word icon in the Dock and select the window of the document you want to switch to.

Switching Documents within Word

1. Windows and macOS Users:
   o In Word, go to View > Switch Windows.
   o A list of open documents will appear. Click on the one you wish to switch to.
2. Alt+Tab (Windows) / Command+Tab (macOS):
   o You can also use keyboard shortcuts like Alt+Tab (Windows) or Command+Tab (macOS) to quickly

toggle between open Word documents and other programs.

Using Multiple Windows

1. To view two documents side by side, go to the View tab, and click View Side by Side.
2. This will allow you to see both documents on the screen at once, making it easier to compare or transfer information.

Chapter 5: Saving and Opening Documents

Save vs. Save As: What's the Difference?

One of the most fundamental skills in using Microsoft Word is knowing how to save your documents. Whether you're saving a new file or updating an existing one, Word provides different ways to handle this.

Save (CTRL + S or Command + S)

- When to Use: Use Save when you've already named your document and are simply updating or making changes to it.
- How it Works: When you select Save, Word saves your document to the current location, keeping the same name and file type.
- Shortcut: Press CTRL + S (Windows) or Command + S (Mac) to quickly save your document.
- Example: If you've been working on a document for a while and make changes, you can save those changes with this option.

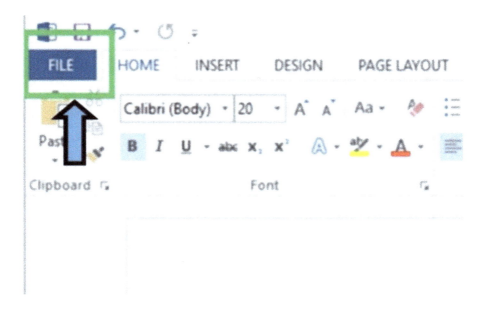

Save As (CTRL + SHIFT + S or Command + SHIFT + S)

- When to Use: Use Save As when you want to save the document in a different location, with a new name, or in a different file format.
- How it Works: You are prompted to choose a new file name and location, and you can select a different file type (e.g., PDF or TXT).
- Example: If you want to save your document under a new name or in a new folder, or if you're saving a copy with edits for someone else, use Save As.

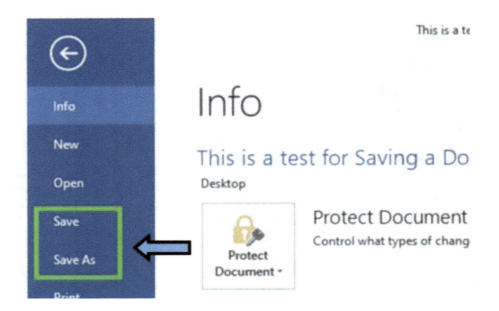

File Formats: DOCX, PDF, TXT, and Others

Microsoft Word supports a variety of file formats, each serving different needs. Understanding these formats is key to managing your documents effectively.

1. DOCX (Microsoft Word Document)

- Default Format: DOCX is the default file format for Word documents. It's the most widely used format for editing and sharing documents in Word.
- How it Works: It retains all your formatting, fonts, images, and other elements. This is the format you'll most commonly work with.
- Example: Save your work regularly as a DOCX file to preserve all features of Word.

2. PDF (Portable Document Format)

- When to Use: Use PDF when you want to share your document without allowing others to edit it. PDFs are ideal for printing or distributing professional documents.
- How it Works: This format preserves the layout, fonts, and images exactly as you see them, but others cannot easily make changes to it.
- Example: If you need to send a final version of your report, save it as a PDF to ensure that it looks the same on any device.

3. TXT (Plain Text)

- When to Use: TXT files are useful when you need a basic document without any formatting or images. These are ideal for transferring content between different types of software or devices.
- How it Works: A TXT file strips out all formatting, meaning no bold, italics, or special fonts will be retained.
- Example: If you want to create a simple text file for transferring to another program or use in a website, save it as a TXT.

4. RTF (Rich Text Format)

- When to Use: RTF files can be opened on nearly any word processor and retain basic formatting like bold, italics, and font changes.
- How it Works: While it doesn't support complex Word features like headers or footers, RTF is a great format for

documents that will be opened on a different system or application.

- Example: If you're working with someone using a different word processor, you might save your document as RTF for compatibility.

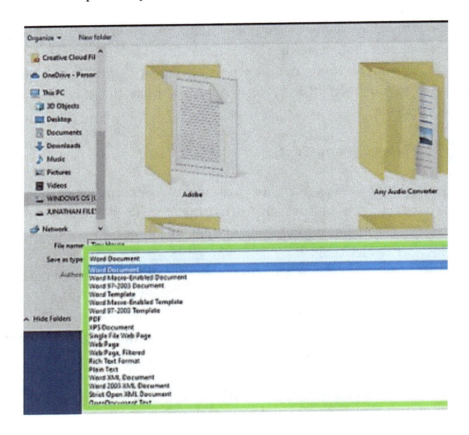

AutoSave and Recovering Unsaved Documents

It's easy to lose your work due to power outages, crashes, or accidental closures. Microsoft Word has built-in AutoSave and document recovery features to protect you.

1. AutoSave

- When It's Active: If you're working on a document saved to OneDrive or SharePoint, AutoSave automatically saves your work every few seconds.
- How it Works: As you type, your changes are saved in real-time, so you never have to worry about losing your progress.
- Example: If your computer crashes, you'll find your document almost exactly as you left it when you reopen Word.

2. Recovering Unsaved Documents

1. If you accidentally close a document without saving, you can recover it using Word's Document Recovery feature.
2. Step-by-Step Recovery:
   - Go to File > Info > Manage Document > Recover Unsaved Documents.
   - Word will display a list of unsaved files. Choose the document you want to recover and click Open.
3. AutoRecover saves versions of your document at regular intervals (every 10 minutes by default). If Word crashes, you'll be prompted to recover the file when you reopen Word.

Organizing Files with Folders

As your collection of Word documents grows, organizing them into folders helps keep everything manageable and easy to find.

Creating Folders

1. Windows:
   - Navigate to File Explorer and choose the location where you want the folder (e.g., Documents, Desktop).
   - Right-click in the area, select New > Folder, and give it a name.
2. macOS:
   - Open Finder, go to the location where you want to create the folder.
   - Right-click and select New Folder, then name it.

Moving Documents into Folders

1. Drag and drop your Word documents into the appropriate folders to keep them organized by project, type, or category.
2. You can also right-click on a document, select Move to or Copy to, and choose the folder.

Using Cloud Storage for Organization

- You can organize your Word documents in cloud storage solutions like OneDrive, Google Drive, or Dropbox.
- These cloud platforms allow you to access your files from any device and keep everything organized in the cloud. Just create folders in the cloud and store your documents accordingly.

Chapter 6: Navigating a Document

As you work in Microsoft Word, efficiently navigating through your document becomes crucial, especially as the size and complexity of your document grow. In this chapter, we'll explore several tools and features that will make moving around a document easy, whether it's a simple page or a lengthy multi-chapter report.

Using Scrollbars and Navigation Panes

When working with a document, one of the most basic ways to navigate is by scrolling through the text. Word provides two main options for scrolling: the scrollbar and the navigation pane.

1. Scrollbars: Basic Navigation

The scrollbar is located on the right side of your document window and allows you to move up and down through your content. You can use the scrollbar to quickly move through the document, especially in long ones.

How it Works:

- Vertical Scrollbar: This allows you to scroll up or down in your document. Click and drag the slider to quickly move to different sections. You can also click the up and down arrows to move one screen at a time.

- Horizontal Scrollbar: This appears at the bottom of the screen when your document extends beyond the current width (for example, in wide tables). Click and drag it to move left or right.

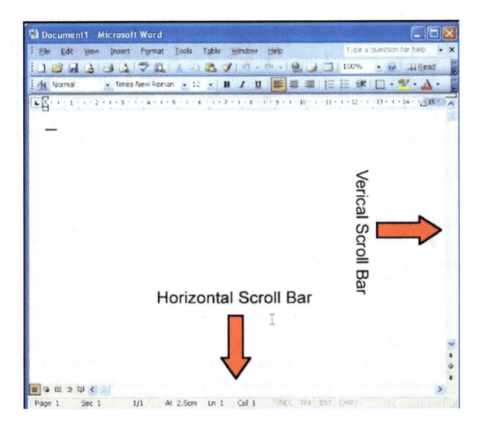

2. Using the Navigation Pane: Advanced Navigation

The Navigation Pane is a powerful tool for quickly moving to specific sections or headings in your document. It's especially helpful for documents that are structured with headings and subheadings.

How to Activate the Navigation Pane:

1. Go to the View tab in the Ribbon.
2. In the Show group, check the box next to Navigation Pane.
3. The Navigation Pane will appear on the left side of the screen, showing a clickable outline of your document's headings.

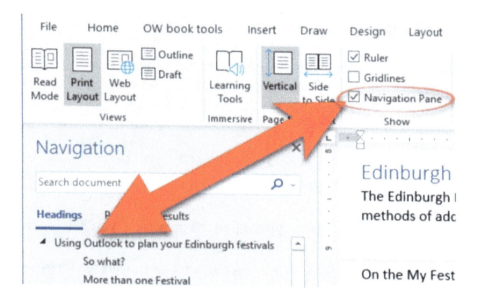

How It Works:

- Headings: If you've used Heading Styles in your document (under the Home tab), they will appear as clickable items in the Navigation Pane. Clicking a heading will jump you directly to that section of the document.
- Search Box: The Navigation Pane also features a search box, where you can type keywords to locate specific parts of your document.

Searching Within a Document Using Find and Replace

Searching through a document becomes easy with the Find and Replace tools, especially in larger documents. These tools let you locate specific text and, in the case of Replace, substitute it with something else.

1. Using Find

The Find function allows you to search for specific words, phrases, or characters in your document, which is very useful for long documents where scrolling might be inefficient.

How to Use Find:

1. Press Ctrl + F (Windows) or Command + F (Mac) to open the Find pane.
2. In the search box, type the word or phrase you are looking for.
3. Word will highlight each occurrence of the search term, and you can use the up and down arrows to navigate through the results.

You can also use Find and Replace on the Home tab under Editing group.

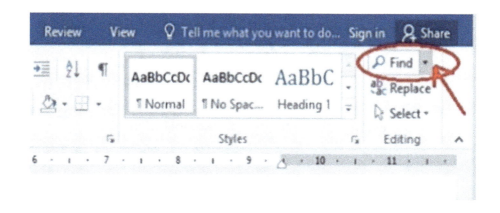

Additional Features:

- Match Case: To search for text exactly as you've typed it (capitalization matters), click the small drop-down arrow in the Find box and select Match Case.
- Find Whole Words Only: This option allows you to search for whole words, not parts of words. For example, searching for "cat" won't highlight "catalog" if you enable this feature.

2. Using Replace

The Replace function allows you to not only find specific text but also replace it with something new. This feature is incredibly useful when you need to change a word, phrase, or formatting throughout the entire document.

How to Use Replace:

1. Press Ctrl + H (Windows) or Command + H (Mac) to open the Find and Replace dialog box.

2. In the Find what field, type the text you want to search for.
3. In the Replace with field, type the text that will replace the old text.
4. Click Find Next to locate the first occurrence. You can then click Replace to swap it out, or click Replace All to change every occurrence of the text in the document.

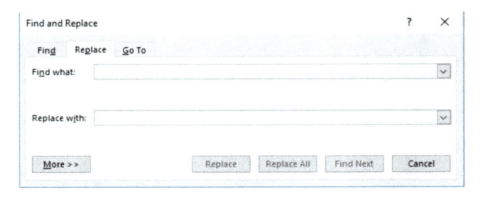

Additional Features in Find and Replace:

- Find Formatting: Click the More button in the Find and Replace dialog box, then select Find Formatting to search for specific formatting (e.g., bold text, font size).
- Replace Formatting: Use Replace Formatting to change the format (e.g., change all instances of a word in italics to regular font style).

Using the Go To Feature

The Go To feature is a powerful tool that lets you jump directly to a specific part of your document without having to manually scroll. It's useful for moving quickly to specific pages, sections, tables, and more.

How to Use Go To:

1. Press Ctrl + G (Windows) or Command + G (Mac), or go to the Home tab, click Find, and then select Go To. Alternatively, you can click on the Home tab. Select the Find dropdown from the Editing group.

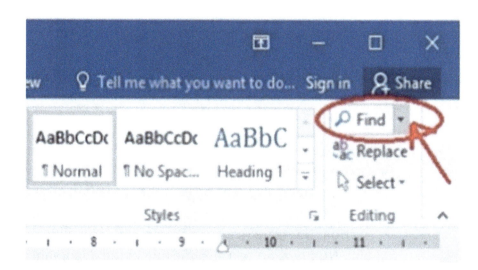

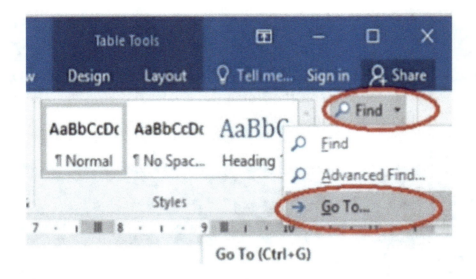

Go To (Ctrl+G)

2. A dialog box will appear where you can enter the following options to jump to a specific location:
    - o Page Number: Type the page number to jump directly to that page.
    - o Section: Navigate to a specific section or heading.
    - o Line Number: Go to a specific line in the document.
    - o Bookmark: Jump to a bookmark you've set in the document (if applicable).
    - o Endnote/Footnote: Move to specific notes in the document.

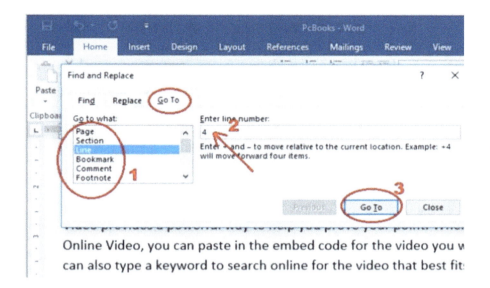

Online Video, you can paste in the embed code for the video you w
can also type a keyword to search online for the video that best fit:

Example:

- If you're working on a large report and need to go straight to
  page 12, use the Go To feature to type in "Page 12" and Word
  will take you there instantly.

Summary: Navigating a Document Efficiently

With these tools—scrollbars, Navigation Pane, Find and Replace,
and Go To—you can quickly move through even the longest and
most complex Word documents. These features save time, increase
productivity, and help you stay organized.

Part 3: Working with Text

Chapter 7: Basic Text Operations

When working in Microsoft Word, the most fundamental actions you'll take are related to manipulating the text in your document. Whether you're typing new content, making changes, or simply moving text around, mastering basic text operations is essential for efficiently creating and editing your documents. In this chapter, we'll cover how to type, delete, select, and manage text, as well as how to use cut, copy, and paste to move or duplicate text. Finally, we'll touch on the Undo and Redo features that allow you to correct mistakes effortlessly.

Typing, Deleting, and Selecting Text

Let's begin with the very basics: entering, removing, and selecting text.

1. Typing Text

Typing in Word is the first step in creating any document. Microsoft Word's interface is designed to make typing as simple and straightforward as possible.

How to Type:

1. Open your document and click anywhere in the document area.

2. Start typing, and Word will insert the text wherever your cursor (blinking vertical line) is positioned.
3. Use the Enter key to start a new line or paragraph.

2. Deleting Text

Deleting text in Microsoft Word is easy, and you can remove text either character by character or in larger chunks, depending on your needs.

Ways to Delete Text:

- Backspace Key: Press the Backspace key to delete the character immediately before the cursor. Holding it down will delete text continuously.
- Delete Key: The Delete key removes the character directly after the cursor. Just like Backspace, holding it down will delete the text continuously.
- Select and Delete: You can also select a portion of text by dragging your mouse over it or using the Shift + arrow keys. Once the text is selected, press Backspace or Delete to remove it.

3. Selecting Text

Selecting text allows you to perform operations like copying, cutting, formatting, or deleting. There are several methods to select text, and you can choose whichever feels easiest for you.

How to Select Text:

- Mouse Method: Click at the beginning of the text you want to select, hold down the left mouse button, and drag across the text. Release the button when you have highlighted the text you want.
- Shift + Arrow Keys: Place the cursor at the start of the text. Hold down the Shift key and use the arrow keys to extend the selection.
- Select All Text: To select all text in the document, press Ctrl + A (Windows) or Command + A (Mac).

Using Cut, Copy, and Paste

These three operations allow you to move or duplicate text within your document or between documents. Understanding how to use these tools effectively will save you a lot of time, especially when reorganizing content.

1. Cut

The Cut function removes selected text from one location and places it on the clipboard, so you can paste it elsewhere in the document.

How to Cut Text:

1. Select the text you want to cut.
2. Right-click on the selected text and choose Cut, or use the keyboard shortcut Ctrl + X (Windows) or Command + X (Mac).
3. Move the cursor to the location where you want to paste the text, and use Ctrl + V (Windows) or Command + V (Mac) to paste it there.

2. Copy

The Copy function creates a duplicate of the selected text and stores it on the clipboard, so you can paste it in another part of the document or even in a different document.

How to Copy Text:

1. Select the text you want to copy.
2. Right-click on the selected text and choose Copy, or use the keyboard shortcut Ctrl + C (Windows) or Command + C (Mac).
3. Move the cursor to the location where you want to paste the text, and press Ctrl + V (Windows) or Command + V (Mac) to paste it.

3. Paste

Once you've used Cut or Copy, the Paste function allows you to insert the text in a new location.

How to Paste Text:

1. Place the cursor where you want the text to be inserted.
2. Right-click and choose Paste, or use the keyboard shortcut Ctrl + V (Windows) or Command + V (Mac).

Paste Options:

- Keep Source Formatting: This option retains the original formatting of the copied or cut text.

- Merge Formatting: This adjusts the formatting of the copied text to match the destination text.
- Keep Text Only: This pastes the text without any formatting (plain text).

You can access these paste options by clicking the small Paste Options button that appears after you paste the text, or by using the Paste drop-down menu in the Home tab.

Undo and Redo: Correcting Mistakes

Mistakes are part of the process when creating a document, and Microsoft Word makes it easy to undo and redo actions so that you can correct them quickly without having to manually erase everything.

1. Undo: Reversing Mistakes

The Undo feature allows you to reverse an action you just performed. If you accidentally deleted text, applied the wrong formatting, or made any unwanted change, Undo will take you back to the previous step.

How to Undo an Action:

1. Click the Undo button in the top-left corner of the window (it looks like a curved arrow pointing left).
2. Or, use the keyboard shortcut Ctrl + Z (Windows) or Command + Z (Mac).

Each click of the Undo button or key press will reverse the last action you performed, one step at a time. You can keep pressing it to undo multiple actions.

2. Redo: Restoring an Action

The Redo function allows you to restore an action that you've undone. If you accidentally reverse something you wanted to keep, simply use the Redo feature to bring it back.

How to Redo an Action:

1. Click the Redo button (next to Undo) in the top-left corner (it looks like a curved arrow pointing right).
2. Or, use the keyboard shortcut Ctrl + Y (Windows) or Command + Y (Mac).

Redo Multiple Actions:

- Just like Undo, you can keep clicking Redo or pressing Ctrl + Y (Windows) to redo multiple actions in succession.

Summary: Mastering Basic Text Operations

Now that you know how to type, delete, select, and move text using Cut, Copy, and Paste, as well as how to use Undo and Redo to correct mistakes, you've got a strong foundation for editing your Word documents. These essential skills will help you maintain control over your text and increase your efficiency.

Chapter 8: Formatting Text

One of the most important aspects of working with Microsoft Word is making your document visually appealing and readable. Formatting text allows you to emphasize key points, make content easier to digest, and create a professional presentation of your ideas. Whether you're adjusting the font style, changing text size, or applying special effects like bold or italics, learning how to format text efficiently is a crucial skill.

In this chapter, we will explore various methods of formatting text, including changing fonts and sizes, applying text effects like bold, italics, underline, and more. We will also cover how to highlight text and create superscripts and subscripts. By the end of this chapter, you'll be able to transform your plain text into a visually striking document.

Changing Fonts, Sizes, and Colors

Changing the font and size of your text helps to create emphasis and structure within your document. You can adjust the text to fit the tone of your writing, whether you're crafting a formal report or an informal blog post.

Changing the Font:

The font is the typeface used to display text. Microsoft Word offers a wide range of fonts, from basic styles like Arial and Times New Roman to more decorative options.

1. Select the text you want to change.
2. Go to the Home tab on the Ribbon.
3. In the Font group, click the drop-down menu for Font to see the available font styles.
4. Scroll through the list or type the name of the font you want to use.
5. Click on the font, and it will be applied to the selected text.

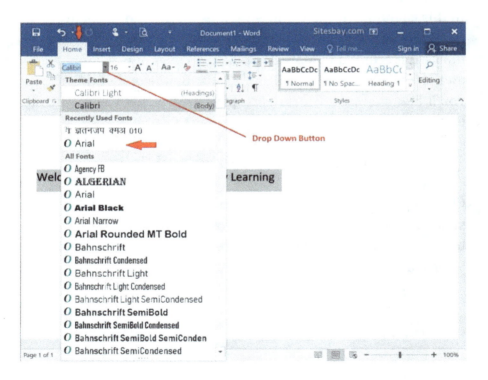

Tip: When selecting a font, keep in mind readability and the purpose of your document. Stick with professional fonts for business documents and creative fonts for more informal or artistic pieces.

Changing the Font Size:

Font size controls the height of the text. Larger sizes are used for headings and titles, while smaller sizes are used for body text.

1. Select the text whose size you want to adjust.
2. On the Home tab, find the Font Size box in the Font group.
3. Click the drop-down arrow next to the font size, and select a size, or type the desired size in the box and press Enter.
4. Alternatively, you can use the Increase Font Size or Decrease Font Size buttons (with the A icon and arrows) to change the size incrementally.

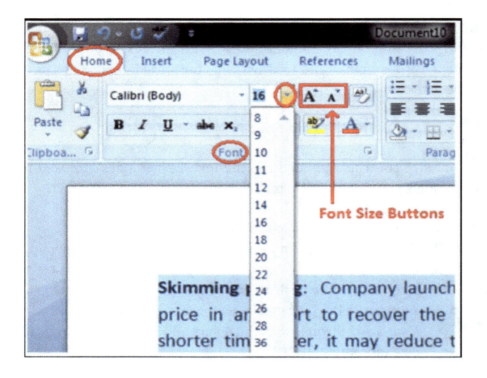

Changing the Font Color:

Changing the color of your text is an effective way to highlight key points, but use this feature sparingly to maintain clarity.

1. Select the text you want to color.
2. In the Home tab, locate the Font Color button (the A with a color bar underneath).
3. Click the drop-down arrow next to it to open the color palette.
4. Select a color, or click More Colors for additional options, including custom colors.

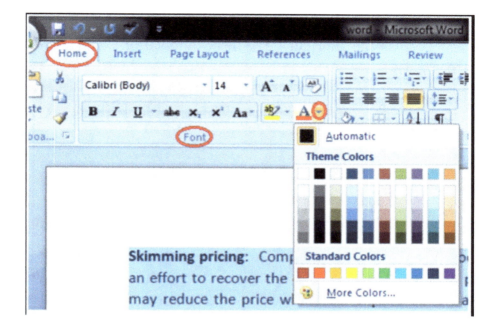

Tip: Stick to a limited color palette to maintain a professional look. Bright, flashy colors are generally not suitable for formal documents.

Applying Bold, Italics, Underline, and Other Effects

Formatting text with bold, italics, underline, and other effects helps highlight important content. These are the basic tools for drawing attention to specific parts of your text.

Bold:

Bold **text** makes characters thicker, helping them stand out in a paragraph.

1. Select the text you want to make bold.

2. In the Home tab, click the Bold button (represented by a B), or use the shortcut Ctrl + B (Windows) or Command + B (Mac).

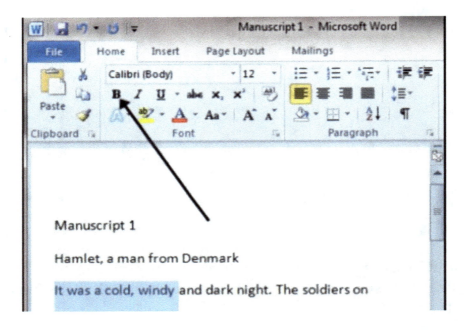

You can also apply bold text by using the Font dialog box for more precise control over bolding specific sections of text.

Italics:

Italicized *text* slants slightly to the right and is commonly used for emphasis, book titles, or foreign words.

1. Select the text you want to italicize.
2. Click the Italics button (represented by an I) in the Home tab, or use the shortcut Ctrl + I (Windows) or Command + I (Mac).

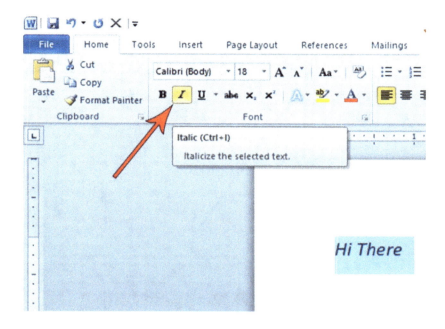

Underline:

Underlining draws a line beneath the underline text and can be used for emphasis, much like bolding.

1. Select the text you want to underline.
2. In the Home tab, click the Underline button (represented by a U) or use the shortcut Ctrl + U (Windows) or Command + U (Mac).

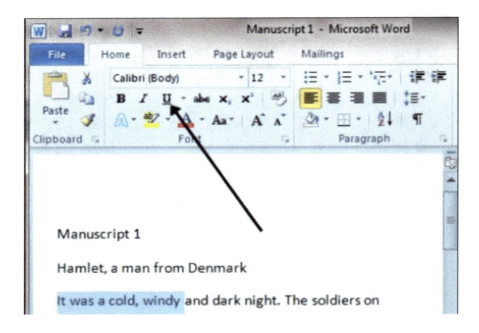

Strikethrough:

Strikethrough applies a line through the middle of the ~~text~~, often used for showing text that has been deleted or to indicate something has been completed.

1. Select the text you want to strike through.
2. In the Home tab, click the Strikethrough button (it looks like a line through the abc).

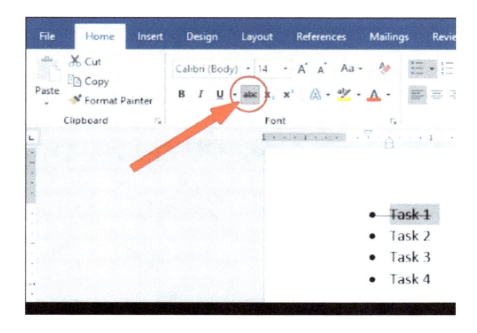

Subscript and Superscript:

Subscript and superscript are often used in mathematical expressions, chemical formulas, or for footnotes. Example is A_2 and A^2

- Subscript: Text appears smaller and below the baseline.
- Superscript: Text appears smaller and above the baseline.

To apply subscript or superscript:

1. Select the text you want to format.
2. Go to the Home tab and click the Subscript or Superscript button in the Font group. The subscript icon looks like a x_2, and the superscript icon looks like a x^2.

You can also use the keyboard shortcuts:

- Subscript: Ctrl + = (Windows) or Command + = (Mac).
- Superscript: Ctrl + Shift + = (Windows) or Command + Shift + = (Mac).

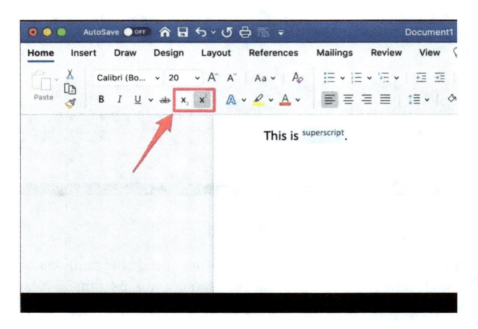

Highlighting Text for Emphasis

Highlighting text is a great way to draw attention to key words, phrases, or sections in your document.

1. Select the text you want to highlight.
2. In the Home tab, find the Text Highlight Color button (it looks like a marker).

3. Click the button to apply the default highlight color (usually yellow), or click the drop-down arrow to choose a different color.

Tip: Use highlighting sparingly—only for key points or when it's essential to draw attention to something specific.

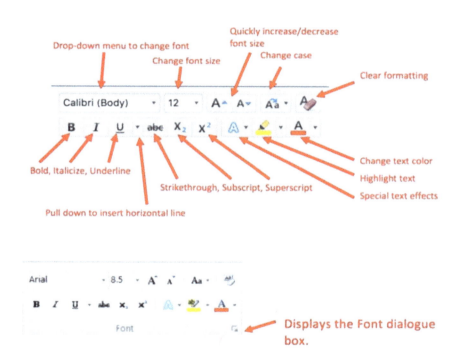

Summary: Mastering Text Formatting

Formatting your text is a powerful way to improve the appearance of your document and make it more engaging. In this chapter, you learned how to change the font, size, and color of text, apply bold, italics, underline, and other text effects, and how to use highlighting, superscripts, and subscripts for specialized content. With these tools at your disposal, you can give your document a professional, polished look that helps convey your message clearly and effectively.

Chapter 9: Paragraph Formatting

Once you have your text in place, it's time to make sure your paragraphs are properly structured and aligned to create a neat and organized document. Paragraph formatting is essential to improving readability and creating a visually appealing layout. In this chapter, we will explore how to adjust paragraph alignment, indent paragraphs, manage line and paragraph spacing, and use bulleted or numbered lists to present information clearly.

By the end of this chapter, you'll have a strong understanding of how to arrange your paragraphs for clarity and impact.

Adjusting Alignment: Left, Center, Right, Justify

Alignment refers to how text is positioned within a paragraph. The default alignment for most documents is left-aligned, but sometimes you may want to center or right-align your text, or even justify it to make it span the width of the page. Let's walk through each of these alignment options.

Left Alignment (Default):

In left-aligned text, the text starts from the left edge of the page, and the right edge is uneven. This is the most common alignment used for body text and is ideal for most general documents.

1. Select the paragraph you want to align.

2. On the Home tab, in the Paragraph group, click the Align Left button (it looks like lines aligned to the left).

Shortcut: You can quickly align text to the left using Ctrl + L (Windows) or Command + L (Mac).

Center Alignment:

Center alignment positions your text in the middle of the page. It's commonly used for titles, headings, and certain types of formal documents.

1. Select the text you want to center.
2. In the Home tab, in the Paragraph group, click the Center button (it looks like lines aligned in the middle).

Shortcut: Quickly center your text using Ctrl + E (Windows) or Command + E (Mac).

Right Alignment:

Right alignment places the text along the right edge of the page, with the left edge uneven. This is often used for certain headings, dates, or specific formats like resumes.

1. Select the paragraph you want to align to the right.
2. In the Home tab, in the Paragraph group, click the Align Right button (it looks like lines aligned to the right).

Shortcut: Quickly right-align your text using Ctrl + R (Windows) or Command + R (Mac).

Justify Alignment:

Justifying your text spreads it across the entire width of the page, making the left and right margins even. This is commonly used for formal documents such as reports, essays, and books.

1. Select the paragraph you want to justify.
2. In the Home tab, in the Paragraph group, click the Justify button (it looks like lines stretched across the page).

Shortcut: To justify your text quickly, use Ctrl + J (Windows) or Command + J (Mac).

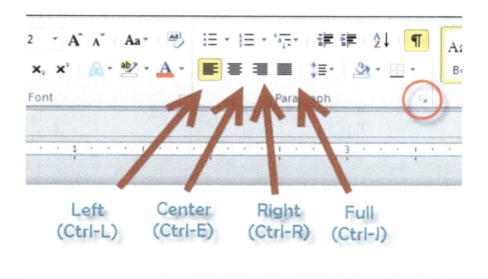

Indenting Paragraphs

Indenting paragraphs is another way to improve the structure of your document. By adding indents, you create a visual separation between paragraphs, making your document easier to read. Word gives you several options for adjusting paragraph indents.

First Line Indent:

A first-line indent is a common way to indicate the start of a new paragraph. It typically involves pushing the first line of a paragraph a bit to the right, while the rest of the paragraph remains aligned with the left margin.

1. Place your cursor at the beginning of the paragraph where you want to apply the indent.
2. In the Home tab, go to the Paragraph group, and click the small dialog box launcher (the small arrow in the corner).
3. In the Paragraph dialog box, under Indentation, select First line from the Special drop-down list.
4. Adjust the By field to set the desired amount of indent. The default is usually 0.5 inches, but you can adjust it to your preference.

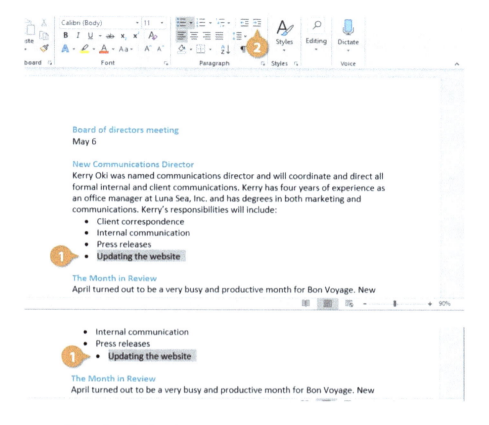

Hanging Indent:

A hanging indent is used when the first line of a paragraph is flush with the left margin, and the following lines are indented. This style is often used for bibliographies or reference lists.

1. Select the paragraph to which you want to apply a hanging indent.
2. In the Home tab, in the Paragraph group, click the dialog box launcher.
3. In the Paragraph dialog box, under Indentation, select Hanging from the Special drop-down list.

4. Adjust the By field to set how much the rest of the paragraph should be indented.

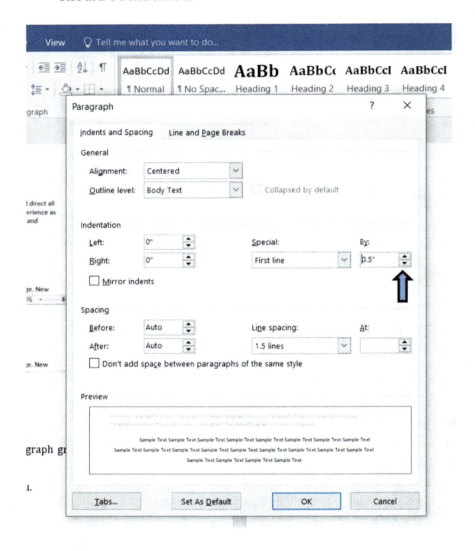

Adding and Managing Line and Paragraph Spacing

Line and paragraph spacing control the amount of space between the lines within a paragraph and between paragraphs themselves. Proper spacing can significantly improve the readability of your document.

Line Spacing:

Line spacing determines the amount of space between individual lines of text. By default, Word uses 1.15 line spacing, but you can adjust this to your preferred spacing.

1. Select the text where you want to change the line spacing.
2. In the Home tab, in the Paragraph group, click the Line and Paragraph Spacing button (it looks like a line with arrows pointing up and down).
3. Choose a spacing option from the list, such as 1.0 for single spacing, 1.5 for 1.5-line spacing, or 2.0 for double spacing.
4. You can also click Line Spacing Options at the bottom of the list to customize the spacing further.

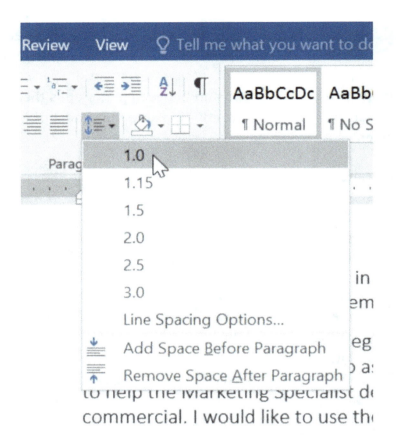

Paragraph Spacing:

Paragraph spacing refers to the amount of space that appears before or after each paragraph.

1. Select the paragraphs you want to modify.
2. In the Home tab, in the Paragraph group, click the Line and Paragraph Spacing button.
3. Select Add Space Before Paragraph or Remove Space After Paragraph to adjust the spacing between paragraphs.

4. Alternatively, click Line Spacing Options to open the Paragraph dialog box, where you can manually adjust the Before and After fields under Spacing.

Creating Bulleted and Numbered Lists

Bulleted and numbered lists are great for organizing information, creating easy-to-read outlines, or breaking up large chunks of text. Let's look at how to create and manage these lists.

Creating a Bulleted List:

Bulleted lists allow you to present information without the need for numbering. This is perfect for lists that don't require a specific order.

1. Place your cursor where you want to start the bulleted list.
2. In the Home tab, in the Paragraph group, click the Bullets button (it looks like three dots with lines).
3. Begin typing your list items. Press Enter to create the next bullet point.
4. To end the list, press Enter twice or click the Bullets button again.

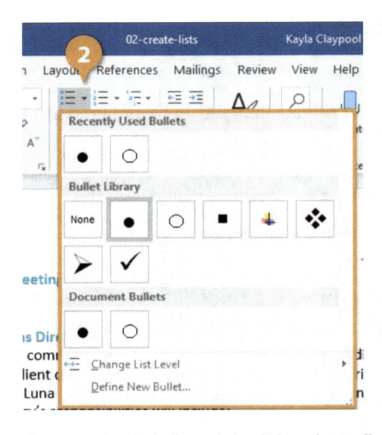

You can also customize the bullet style by clicking the small arrow next to the Bullets button and selecting Define New Bullet.

Creating a Numbered List:

Numbered lists are ideal when you need to present information in a specific order, such as instructions or steps in a process.

1. Place your cursor where you want to start the numbered list.
2. In the Home tab, in the Paragraph group, click the Numbering button (it looks like numbers 1, 2, 3).

3. Start typing your list items and press Enter to create the next numbered item.
4. To end the list, press Enter twice or click the Numbering button again.

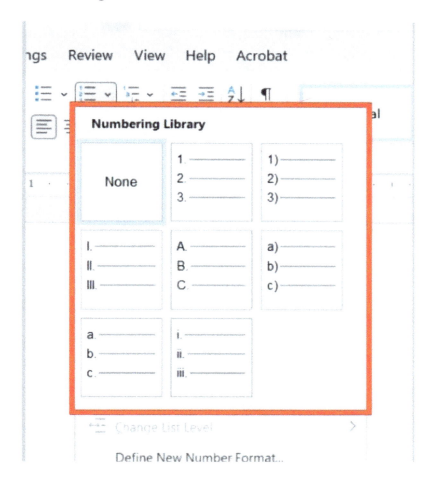

You can also customize the numbering style by clicking the small arrow next to the Numbering button and selecting Define New Number Format.

Summary: Mastering Paragraph Formatting

In this chapter, we've learned how to format paragraphs in Microsoft Word by adjusting alignment, adding indents, and managing line and paragraph spacing. Additionally, we explored how to create and customize bulleted and numbered lists, which are excellent tools for organizing content. Mastering paragraph formatting will help you create well-structured and easy-to-read documents that flow smoothly and look professional.

Part 4: Enhancing Your Document

Chapter 10: Page Layout and Design

A well-designed document isn't just about the content—it's also about how that content is presented on the page. In this chapter, we'll explore the tools that allow you to adjust the overall layout and design of your document. From setting up margins and orientation to adding headers and footers, you'll learn how to give your document a professional and polished appearance.

By the end of this chapter, you'll have a strong grasp on page layout features and how to make your document visually engaging and easy to navigate.

Adjusting Margins, Orientation, and Page Size

Page layout settings such as margins, orientation, and page size affect the way content is arranged on the page. These settings are critical in ensuring your document fits the desired format, especially for printed documents.

Adjusting Margins:

Margins control the space between the content of your document and the edges of the page. The default margin is usually 1 inch, but you can change this to suit your needs, especially if you are preparing a formal document or something to be printed.

1.   Go to the Layout tab on the Ribbon.

2. In the Page Setup group, click on Margins.
3. A dropdown menu will appear with several options, such as Normal, Narrow, Moderate, and Wide.

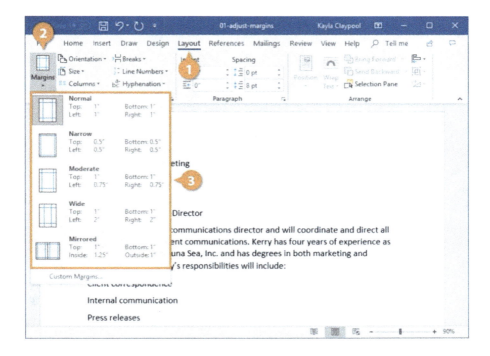

4. To create custom margins, click Custom Margins... at the bottom of the dropdown. In the Page Setup dialog box, you can adjust the top, bottom, left, and right margins as needed.

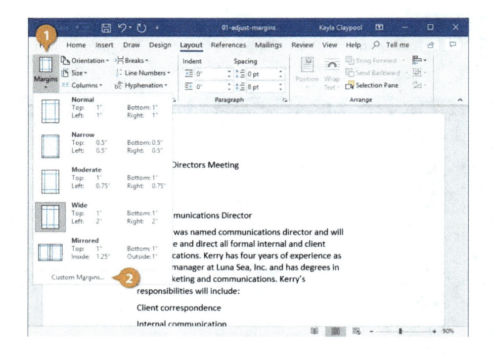

Directors Meeting

munications Director

was named communications director and will
e and direct all formal internal and client
cations. Kerry has four years of experience as
manager at Luna Sea, Inc. and has degrees in
keting and communications. Kerry's
responsibilities will include:

Client correspondence

Internal communication

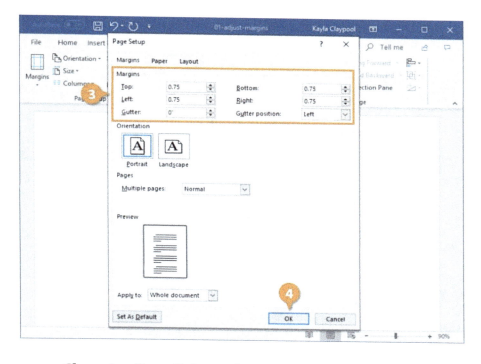

Changing Page Orientation:

Page orientation refers to whether the document is printed in portrait (vertical) or landscape (horizontal) mode. Portrait is the default, but for documents like presentations, spreadsheets, or posters, landscape might be more appropriate.

1. Go to the Layout tab on the Ribbon.
2. In the Page Setup group, click Orientation.
3. Select Portrait or Landscape, depending on your needs.

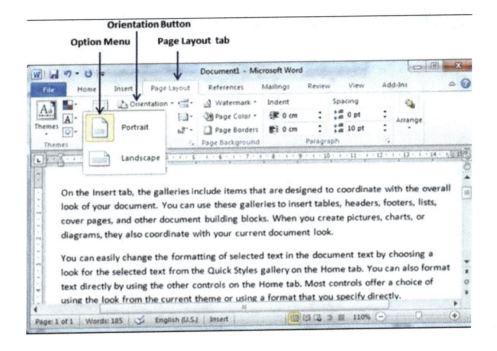

On the Insert tab, the galleries include items that are designed to coordinate with the overall look of your document. You can use these galleries to insert tables, headers, footers, lists, cover pages, and other document building blocks. When you create pictures, charts, or diagrams, they also coordinate with your current document look.

You can easily change the formatting of selected text in the document text by choosing a look for the selected text from the Quick Styles gallery on the Home tab. You can also format text directly by using the other controls on the Home tab. Most controls offer a choice of using the look from the current theme or using a format that you specify directly.

Adjusting Page Size:

The default page size is Letter (8.5 x 11 inches) in the U.S. But if you're working with international documents, you might need A4 size or a custom size. Word allows you to change this easily.

1. Go to the Layout tab.
2. In the Page Setup group, click Size.
3. Select a predefined page size (e.g., A4, Legal, Tabloid).
4. For a custom size, click More Paper Sizes at the bottom of the dropdown, and enter the desired dimensions in the Page Setup dialog box.

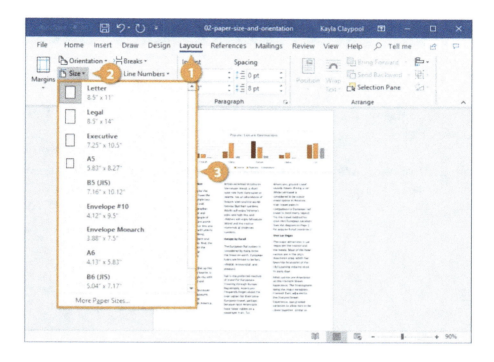

Setting Up Headers and Footers

Headers and footers are areas in the top and bottom margins of the page where you can place text or graphics that will appear on every page (or select pages) in your document. They are commonly used for page numbers, document titles, author names, dates, and logos.

Adding a Header:

A header appears at the top of each page, and it's often used for things like titles or chapter headings.

1. Double-click in the Header area at the top of the page. Alternatively, go to the Insert tab and click Header.

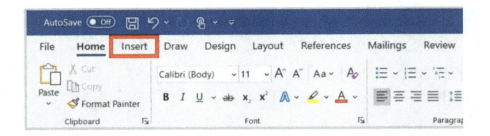

2. Choose a preformatted header style from the list or click Edit Header to create your own.

3. Type the content you want to appear in the header (e.g., document title, chapter name, etc.).
4. When you're done, click Close Header and Footer on the Ribbon, or double-click outside the header area.

Adding a Footer:

Footers appear at the bottom of the page, and they are commonly used for page numbers, dates, or author names.

1. Double-click in the Footer area at the bottom of the page. Alternatively, go to the Insert tab and click Footer.
2. Choose a preformatted footer style or select Edit Footer to customize it.
3. Type in the information you want to appear in the footer, such as document version, copyright information, or author's name.
4. Click Close Header and Footer when finished, or double-click outside the footer area.

Customizing Headers and Footers:

1. In the Header & Footer Tools design tab, you can adjust the layout, align text, and add elements like page numbers or dates.
2. To add a page number, go to Header & Footer Tools, click Page Number, and choose from the options: Top of Page, Bottom of Page, or Page Margins.
3. If you want different headers or footers on odd and even pages (for example, to have the page number on the right for odd pages and on the left for even pages), check the box labeled Different Odd & Even Pages under Header & Footer Tools.
4. You can also create a First Page header or footer by checking the box labeled Different First Page under Header & Footer

Tools. This is useful for excluding a header or footer on the first page of a document (e.g., title pages).

Adding Page Numbers

Page numbers are typically placed in the header or footer of a document to help readers keep track of their position in the document. Word makes it easy to add page numbers in a variety of formats.

1. Go to the Insert tab on the Ribbon.

2. In the Header & Footer group, click Page Number.
3. Choose the location for your page numbers (Top of Page, Bottom of Page, Page Margins).

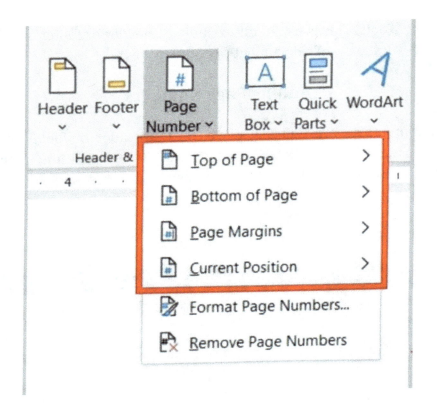

4. Select the page number style you prefer.

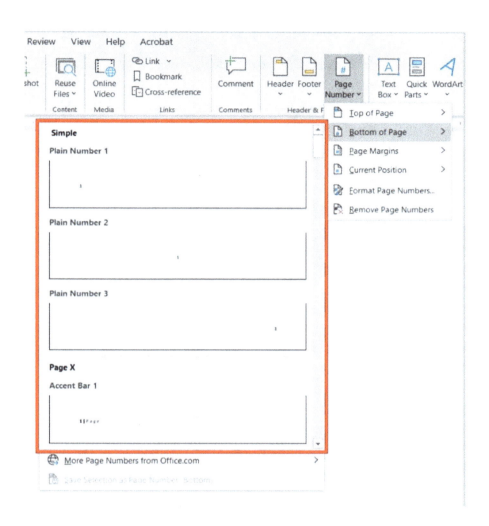

5. If you want to change the starting page number (e.g., if your document begins on a page other than 1), click **Format Page Numbers** and choose a starting number.

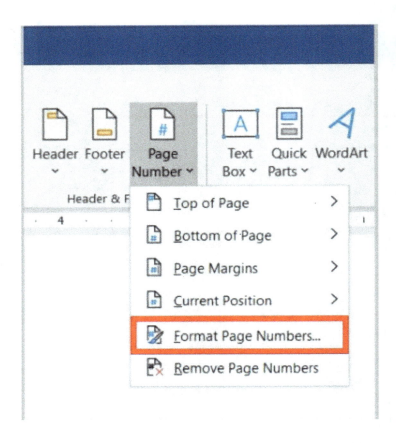

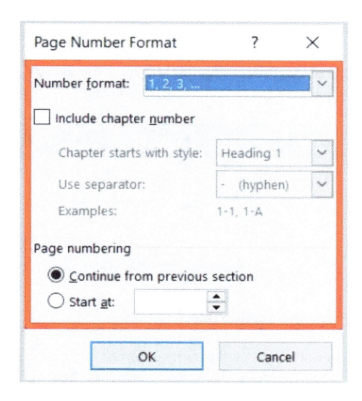

Working with Section Breaks and Page Breaks

Section breaks and page breaks are powerful tools that allow you to organize your document more precisely. Section breaks let you divide your document into parts, each with its own formatting, such as different headers, footers, or page numbering. Page breaks ensure content starts on a new page, which is particularly useful in long documents.

Inserting a Page Break:

A page break forces the content to start from a new page, without affecting the layout or formatting of the current section.

1. Place your cursor where you want the page to break.
2. Go to the Insert tab, and in the Pages group, click Page Break.
3. Alternatively, you can press Ctrl + Enter (Windows) or Command + Enter (Mac) to insert a page break quickly.

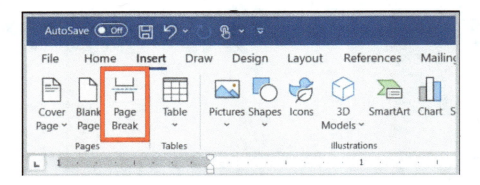

Inserting a Section Break:

A section break allows you to apply different formatting settings to different parts of your document, such as changing the page orientation for a section, or creating different headers and footers.

1. Place your cursor where you want the new section to begin.
2. Go to the Layout tab on the Ribbon.

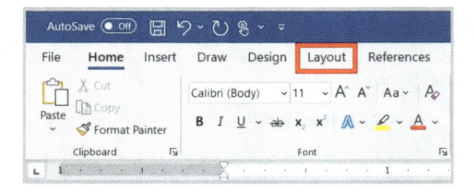

3. In the Page Setup group, click Breaks.

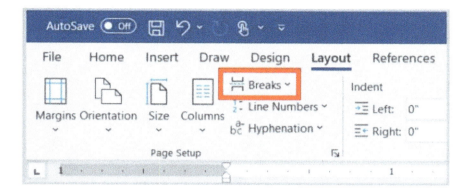

4. Under Section Breaks, choose the appropriate break type:
    o   Next Page: Starts the new section on the next page.
    o   Continuous: Starts the new section on the same page.
    o   Even Page: Starts the new section on the next even-numbered page.
    o   Odd Page: Starts the new section on the next odd-numbered page.

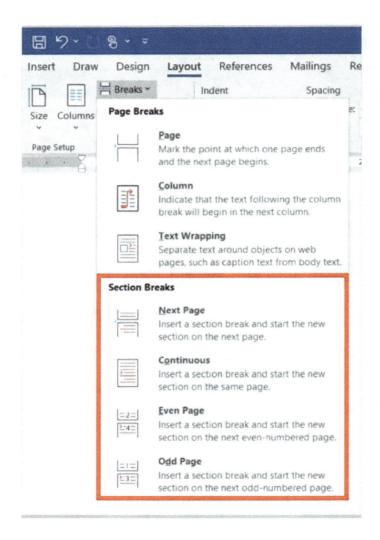

Summary: Mastering Page Layout and Design

In this chapter, you've learned how to set up your document's overall appearance by adjusting margins, page orientation, and page size. You also explored how to add and customize headers and footers, which are essential for professional-looking documents.

Furthermore, we covered how to insert page numbers and make your document easy to navigate with page and section breaks.

Mastering page layout and design in Microsoft Word is crucial for creating polished, readable, and well-structured documents. As you continue your journey, these layout tools will help you ensure that your content is both professional and visually appealing.

Chapter 11: Tables

Tables are an essential tool for organizing information in a structured and easy-to-read format. Whether you're creating a report, a budget, or a schedule, tables help break down complex data into a more digestible format. In this chapter, we'll walk you through the steps of creating, modifying, and styling tables in Microsoft Word.

By the end of this chapter, you'll be able to confidently create tables, add or remove rows and columns, merge and split cells, and apply professional-looking table styles to make your documents more polished and accessible.

Creating a Table from Scratch

Creating a table in Word is quick and straightforward. You can manually insert rows and columns or use Word's automatic table generation tools. Here's how to create a basic table from scratch:

Step-by-Step Instructions:

1. Position the cursor where you want the table to appear in your document.
2. Go to the Insert tab on the Ribbon.
3. In the Tables group, click Table.

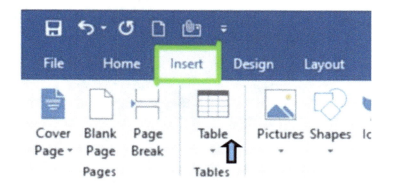

4. A dropdown menu will appear with a grid. Drag your cursor over the grid to select the number of rows and columns you want for your table (e.g., 3x3 for a table with three rows and three columns).

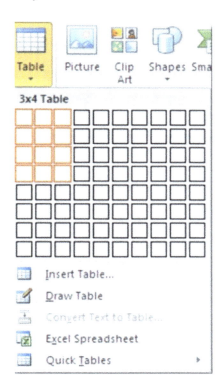

Alternatively, click Insert Table at the bottom of the dropdown for more precise control over the number of rows and columns.

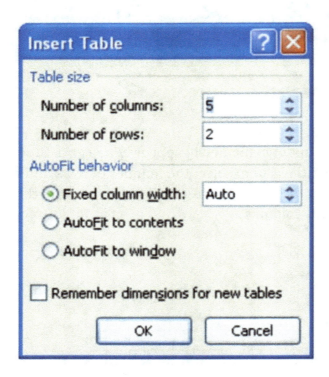

5. Once the grid is selected, click to insert the table. Word will automatically generate a table with the selected dimensions.

Tip: You can also create a table by typing out the structure using Tab and Enter. Word will automatically convert it into a table after you type in the appropriate number of columns and rows and press Enter.

Adding and Removing Rows/Columns

Once your table is inserted, you may need to modify it by adding or removing rows or columns based on your content needs. Let's walk through how to make these adjustments.

Adding Rows and Columns:

1. To add a row:
   - Right-click on the row where you want to insert a new one (either above or below).
   - In the context menu, hover over Insert, and choose:
     - Insert Rows Above to add a row above the selected row.
     - Insert Rows Below to add a row below the selected row.
2. To add a column:
   - Right-click on the column where you want to insert a new one (either to the left or right).
   - In the context menu, hover over Insert, and choose:
     - Insert Columns to the Left to add a column to the left of the selected column.
     - Insert Columns to the Right to add a column to the right of the selected column.

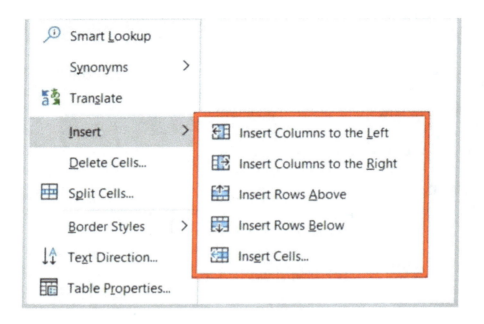

Removing Rows and Columns:

1. To remove a row:
   - Right-click the row you wish to delete.
   - From the context menu, choose Delete Row.
2. To remove a column:
   - Right-click the column you wish to delete.
   - From the context menu, choose Delete Column.

Merging and Splitting Cells

Merging cells is a great way to combine two or more cells into one larger cell, ideal for creating headers or emphasizing a specific section of the table. Splitting cells is useful when you want to divide one cell into multiple smaller cells.

Merging Cells:

1. Select the cells you want to merge. You can click and drag to highlight multiple cells in the table.
2. Once the cells are selected, right-click and choose Merge Cells from the context menu, or go to the Table Tools Layout tab on the Ribbon.
3. In the Merge group, click Merge Cells.

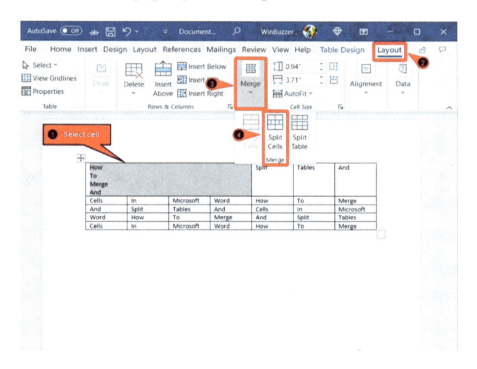

Splitting Cells:

1. Select the cell you want to split.

2. Right-click the selected cell and choose Split Cells from the context menu, or go to the Table Tools Layout tab and click Split Cells.
3. In the Split Cells dialog box, choose how many columns and rows you want to divide the cell into, and then click OK.

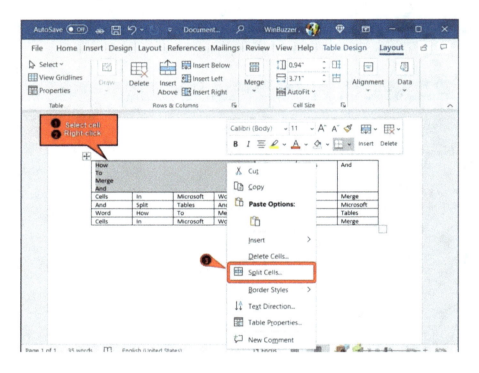

Applying Table Styles for a Professional Look

Word offers a range of pre-designed table styles that you can apply to quickly enhance the visual appeal of your table. These styles include different color schemes, border options, and shading that can give your table a professional appearance in just a few clicks.

Applying a Table Style:

1. Click anywhere inside the table you've created.
2. Go to the Table Tools Design tab, which appears once the table is selected.
3. In the Table Styles group, you'll see a variety of pre-set table designs. Hover over the different styles to preview them.
4. Click on a style to apply it to your table. Word will automatically format the table with the selected style.

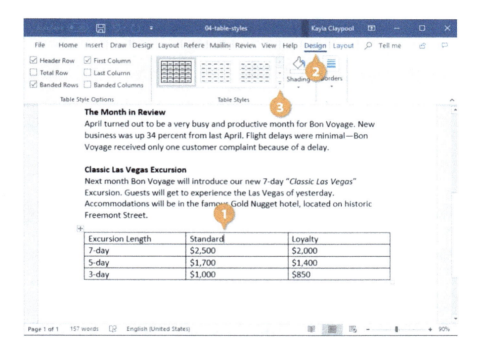

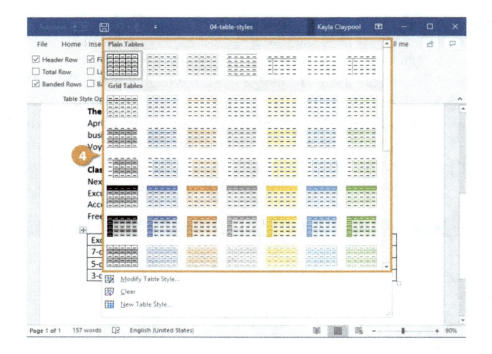

Customizing a Table Style:

While Word offers predefined styles, you can also create a custom look by modifying aspects like borders, shading, and font styles.

1. Click anywhere inside the table.
2. Go to the Table Tools Design tab.
3. In the Table Styles group, click Shading to change the background color of cells or rows.
4. Click Borders to adjust the border style, color, and width.
5. To modify the font, highlight the text in the table and apply formatting from the Home tab, such as changing the font, size, or color.

Alternating Row Colors (Banding):

To make tables easier to read, especially when you have a lot of data, you can apply banded rows (alternating row colors) for better contrast.

1. In the Table Tools Design tab, check the box labeled Banded Rows under Table Style Options.
2. This will alternate the row colors to make your table more readable. You can also toggle Banded Columns if you prefer alternating colors in the columns instead.

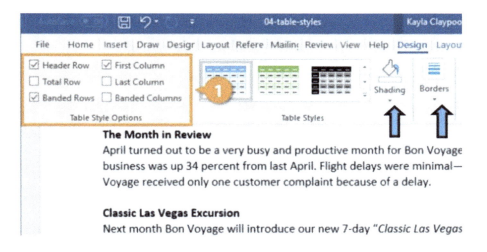

Bonus Tip: Using Table for Forms and Surveys

Tables aren't just for organizing text and numbers—they can also be useful for creating forms or surveys. You can use tables to create grids for checkboxes, radio buttons, or text fields. Simply insert a table with as many rows and columns as you need, and in each cell, you can insert checkboxes or text fields to gather information.

Summary: Mastering Tables for Professional Documents

Tables are a powerful tool for organizing and presenting information clearly and effectively. In this chapter, we learned how to create a table from scratch, modify it by adding or removing rows and columns, and merge or split cells for better layout. We also explored how to apply professional table styles and customize them to fit your document's needs.

Mastering tables will allow you to create everything from data-driven reports to neatly organized schedules and forms. By using these techniques, you can take your documents to the next level in terms of clarity, organization, and professionalism.

Chapter 12: Adding Visual Elements

Visual elements can transform a plain text document into a more engaging and professional piece of work. Whether you're creating a presentation, a report, or just adding a touch of creativity to a letter, incorporating pictures, shapes, icons, and SmartArt can significantly enhance your document's appeal and readability. In this chapter, we'll cover the essential techniques for inserting and formatting various visual elements in Microsoft Word.

By the end of this chapter, you'll be able to add images, shapes, and SmartArt effectively, resize and format them to fit your document, and apply text wrapping to control how text interacts with these visual elements.

Inserting Pictures and Online Images

Adding pictures to your document is an easy way to bring your content to life. Whether you're inserting images from your computer or using online resources, Word makes it simple to incorporate visuals into your documents.

Step-by-Step Instructions:

1. Inserting Pictures from Your Computer:
    o Place the cursor where you want the picture to appear.

- Go to the Insert tab on the Ribbon.
- In the Illustrations group, click Pictures.
- Choose This Device to browse and select an image saved on your computer.

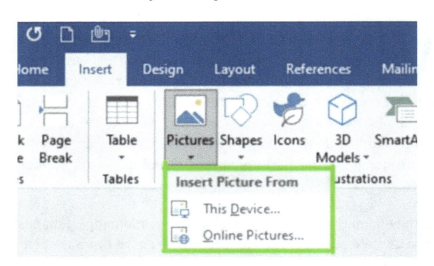

- Click Insert to add the picture to your document.

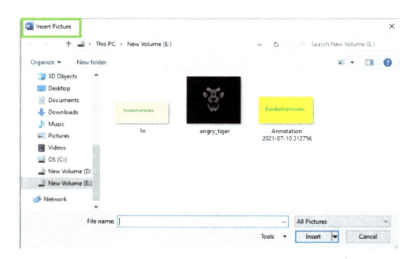

2. Inserting Online Images:
   - Place the cursor where you want the image.
   - Go to the Insert tab.
   - In the Illustrations group, click Online Pictures.
   - A window will open where you can search for images from Bing or insert images from OneDrive.
   - Once you find the image you want, click on it, then select Insert.

Tip: If you're using images from the web, ensure that they are royalty-free or that you have permission to use them, especially for commercial purposes.

Adding Shapes, Icons, and SmartArt

Shapes, icons, and SmartArt are perfect for adding more graphical content to your document. These tools allow you to create flowcharts, diagrams, and stylish elements to communicate information in a visual way.

Adding Shapes:

1. Place your cursor where you want the shape to appear.
2. Go to the Insert tab and click Shapes in the Illustrations group.

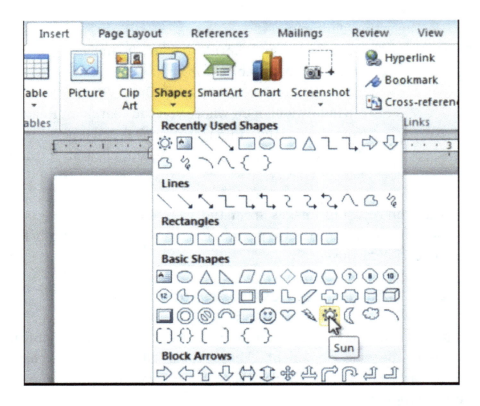

3. A dropdown menu will appear with different shape options like rectangles, circles, arrows, and lines.
4. Select the shape you want and click and drag on the document to draw it.
5. To resize the shape, click on the shape to activate its handles and drag the handles to adjust the size.

Adding Icons:

1. Place your cursor where you want the icon.
2. Go to the Insert tab and click Icons in the Illustrations group.
3. In the Icons window, browse or search for the icon you want to insert.

4. Select the icon, then click Insert to add it to the document.
5. Resize or rotate the icon as needed.

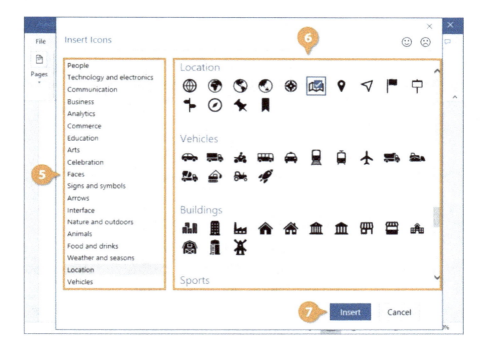

Adding SmartArt:

SmartArt allows you to create diagrams and visuals for lists, processes, hierarchies, and more. Here's how to add it:

1. Place your cursor where you want the SmartArt graphic to appear.
2. Go to the Insert tab and click SmartArt in the Illustrations group.

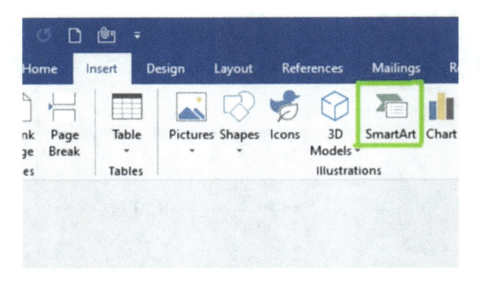

3. The Choose a SmartArt Graphic dialog box will open. Browse the categories or use the search bar to find the appropriate type (e.g., Process, Hierarchy, Relationship).
4. Select the graphic that fits your needs, and click OK to insert it.

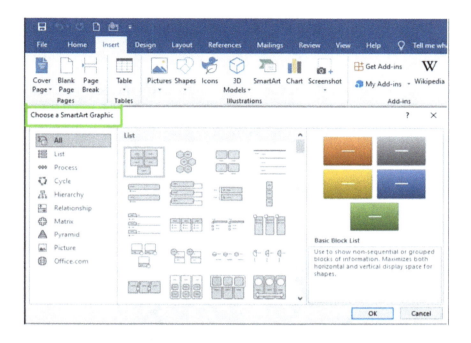

5. Customize the SmartArt by typing in the text fields, changing the colors, and adjusting the layout as needed.

Formatting and Resizing Images

Once you have added images, shapes, icons, or SmartArt to your document, it's essential to format them to fit the layout and style of your document.

Resizing Images:

1. Select the image (or shape, icon, SmartArt).
2. Once selected, small handles will appear around the image.

3. To resize, click and drag one of the handles. To maintain the aspect ratio (proportional resizing), hold the Shift key while dragging the corner handle.
4. Alternatively, you can right-click the image, select Size and Position, and enter specific width and height values in the dialog box for precise resizing.

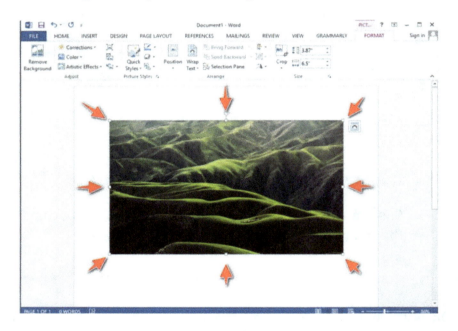

Formatting Images:

1. Click on the image you want to format.
2. Go to the Picture Tools Format tab that appears on the Ribbon when an image is selected.
3. In the Adjust group, you can use the Corrections (for brightness/contrast), Color (to adjust hues or apply effects), and Artistic Effects buttons to modify the image's appearance.

4. To add borders or effects to your image, use the Picture Border and Picture Effects dropdown menus.

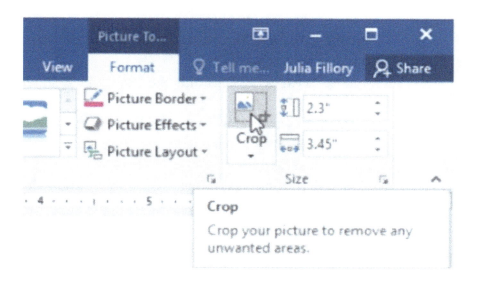

Tip: If you want to add a shadow, glow, or reflection to your images, the Picture Effects menu is an excellent tool to give your images a professional look.

Using Text Wrapping for Better Layout

Text wrapping allows you to control how the text interacts with visual elements. Instead of having the text bunch up around your images or shapes, text wrapping ensures that your images and text flow around each other neatly. There are several ways you can wrap text around an image or shape.

Changing Text Wrapping:

1. Select the image, shape, or SmartArt you want to adjust.

2. Right-click the object, and in the context menu, click Wrap Text. Alternatively, with the image selected, on the Format tab, click Wrap Text.
3. You will see several options:
    o In Line with Text: The object is treated as a part of the text, like a letter or a word.
    o Square: Text wraps around the object in a square shape.
    o Tight: Text wraps closely around the object.
    o Through: Text flows around the object, but can also appear inside it.
    o Top and Bottom: Text appears only above and below the object, not to the sides.
    o Behind Text: The object appears behind the text, which can be useful for watermarks.
    o In Front of Text: The object appears in front of the text.
4. Choose the option that best suits your needs. For example, Square and Tight are popular choices for ensuring that the text flows nicely around the image.

Aligning and Moving Visual Elements:

1. Select the image or shape.
2. In the Picture Tools Format or Drawing Tools Format tab, use the Align button in the Arrange group to align the object to the left, center, or right of the page.
3. You can also use the Position button to choose a predefined position for your image or shape on the page.

4. To move the image or object, click and drag it to the desired location. Hold down Shift to move it in straight lines (horizontally or vertically).

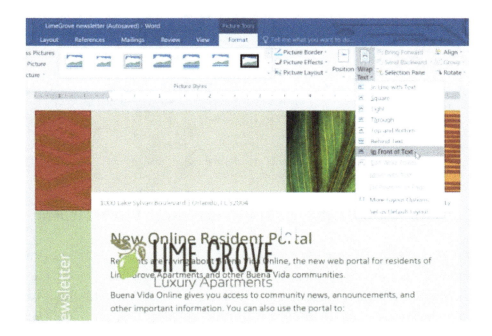

Bonus Tip: Using the Layout Options Button

If you need quick adjustments for text wrapping, you can use the Layout Options button that appears next to an image or shape when it's selected. This button gives you the option to quickly choose the text wrapping style and adjust alignment.

Summary: Enhancing Documents with Visual Elements

In this chapter, we've covered the process of inserting and formatting visual elements like pictures, shapes, icons, and SmartArt. These elements are powerful tools for making your documents more engaging, visually appealing, and professional. We've also explored the techniques for resizing, formatting, and wrapping text around images to ensure your document has a polished and organized appearance.

Part 5: Advanced Features for Beginners

Chapter 13: Templates and Styles

Templates and styles are invaluable tools in Microsoft Word that help you maintain consistency, save time, and create professional-looking documents with minimal effort. Templates provide a framework for different types of documents, while styles allow you to apply predefined formatting to text and other elements in your document. In this chapter, we will explore how to use templates and styles to create polished and consistent documents efficiently.

By the end of this chapter, you'll have the skills to work with Word's pre-designed templates, create your own custom templates, and apply and modify styles to streamline your formatting process.

Exploring Pre-Designed Templates

Microsoft Word comes with a wide variety of pre-designed templates that help you start your documents quickly, with professional formatting already in place. Templates are available for a range of document types, including resumes, reports, letters, brochures, and more.

Step-by-Step Instructions:

1. Accessing Templates:
   o Open Microsoft Word.

- On the Home screen (or the File tab if you're starting a new document), you will see a variety of template categories.
- To browse available templates, click on New from the File tab.
- A window will open showing various templates like Blank Document, Resumes, Letters, Reports, and Brochures. You can search for templates by keyword or browse through the categories.

2. Selecting and Using a Template:
   - Scroll through the template options or use the search bar to find a specific template.
   - When you find one you like, click on it to see a preview.
   - Click Create to open a new document based on the selected template. The template will automatically load with sample text, headings, and formatting already in place.

3. Customizing the Template:
   - Once your template is open, you can replace the sample text with your own content.
   - You can also modify elements like images, tables, and headings. Keep in mind that templates are fully editable, so feel free to adjust any part of the template to suit your needs.

Tip: Templates are not only great for saving time, but they also ensure consistency in document structure and style. If you're working on a large project, such as a report or thesis, templates help maintain uniformity throughout your document.

Creating and Saving Custom Templates

Creating a custom template allows you to save a document design that you use regularly, so you don't have to reformat each time. Whether it's for a company report, a project proposal, or your personal letterhead, custom templates allow you to preserve your unique formatting and structure.

Step-by-Step Instructions:

1. Creating a Custom Template:
   - Open a blank document or start with a pre-designed template that you wish to modify.
   - Format the document as you like, adjusting fonts, colors, margins, headings, and adding any other elements you typically use (like a logo or footer).
   - For example, you can set up a letter template with your address at the top, preferred font and size for the body text, and a signature line at the bottom.
2. Saving the Document as a Template:
   - Once you've customized the document to your liking, click on File in the Ribbon.
   - Choose Save As, then select the location where you want to save the template (e.g., a folder or OneDrive).
   - In the Save as type dropdown menu, select Word Template (.dotx). This file format ensures that you can reuse the template in the future without overwriting it.
   - Enter a name for your template, then click Save.
3. Accessing Your Custom Template:

o   To use your custom template, go to File > New, then click Personal to see templates you've created or saved. You can select your custom template and begin working with it as a new document.

Tip: You can create multiple custom templates for different purposes. If you regularly write reports, resumes, or newsletters, setting up these templates in advance will save you a lot of time.

Applying and Modifying Styles

Styles in Microsoft Word are predefined combinations of fonts, sizes, colors, and other formatting elements that allow you to quickly apply consistent formatting to text throughout your document. Using styles helps ensure uniformity and saves time, especially in longer documents.

Step-by-Step Instructions:

1. Applying Built-in Styles:
    o   Select the text you want to apply a style to (such as a heading or body text).
    o   Go to the Home tab in the Ribbon, and in the Styles group, you'll see several predefined styles like Heading 1, Heading 2, Normal, etc.
    o   Simply click on the desired style, and it will be applied to your selected text. For example, if you apply Heading 1, the text will be formatted with a larger font size, bold weight, and other settings specified for headings.

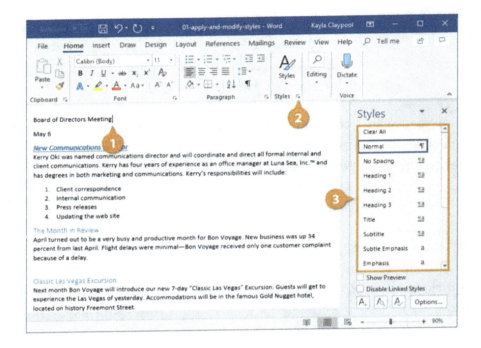

2. Using the Styles Pane for More Options:
   o For additional styles or to customize the styles further, click the Styles Pane button at the bottom right corner of the Styles group on the Home tab.
   o The Styles Pane will open, showing all available styles and offering options for applying, modifying, or creating new styles.
   o You can click the small arrow next to a style name to open more options, such as Modify, Delete, or Add to Quick Style Gallery.
3. Modifying a Style:
   o If you want to modify a style, right-click the style name in the Styles Pane and choose Modify.

- In the Modify Style dialog box, you can adjust font type, size, color, paragraph alignment, line spacing, and more.
- You can also choose whether you want the style to apply to the current document or all documents based on the template.
- After modifying the style, click OK to save your changes. The updated style will automatically apply to all text in the document that uses that style.

Tip: Styles can be especially useful for organizing your document and ensuring that headings, subheadings, and body text follow a consistent format throughout, even if you're working on a large project like a research paper or an eBook.

Bonus Tip: Creating Custom Styles

If you find that the built-in styles don't meet your needs, you can create your own custom styles. Here's how:

1. Select the text that you want to use as the basis for your custom style.
2. Go to the Styles Pane, and at the bottom, click New Style.
3. In the Create New Style from Formatting dialog box, name your style and customize it with your desired settings for font, color, spacing, and more.
4. Click OK to create and save the new style.
5. Your new style will now appear in the Styles group, and you can apply it to other text in your document.

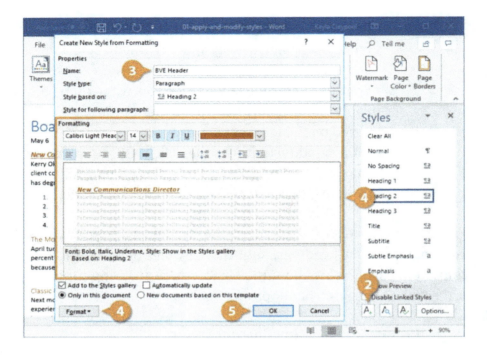

Summary: Enhancing Productivity with Templates and Styles

Templates and styles are essential tools for creating professional and consistent documents quickly and easily. Templates save you time by providing pre-designed layouts, while styles ensure uniformity across your text. By learning how to work with both, you'll be able to focus on the content of your document rather than spending time on repetitive formatting tasks.

Chapter 14: Using Word for Collaboration

In today's fast-paced, connected world, collaboration is key to completing projects efficiently and effectively. Microsoft Word offers several powerful tools to help you collaborate with others, whether you're working on a shared document with colleagues, reviewing a draft, or receiving feedback. In this chapter, we'll dive into the various collaboration features in Microsoft Word, such as adding and managing comments, using Track Changes for edits, and sharing documents for real-time collaboration.

By the end of this chapter, you'll have the skills to seamlessly work with others, keeping your documents organized and up-to-date while gathering feedback and making necessary changes quickly.

Adding and Managing Comments

Comments are a great way to provide feedback, ask questions, or leave reminders within a document without altering the original text. They allow collaborators to share thoughts without interrupting the flow of the content.

Step-by-Step Instructions:

1. Inserting a Comment:
   o Select the text or place in the document where you want to insert a comment.

- Go to the Review tab in the Ribbon.
- Click on New Comment in the Comments group. A comment box will appear in the right margin, where you can type your feedback or notes.

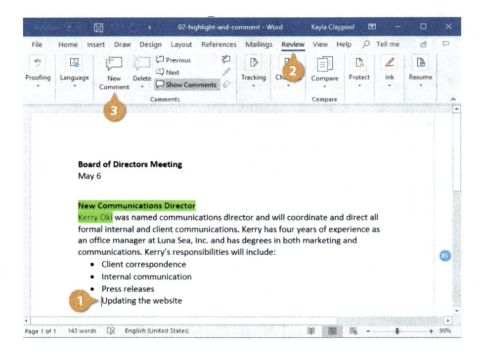

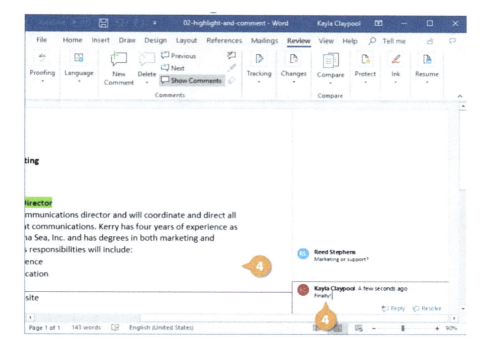

2. Viewing and Navigating Comments:
   - To see all comments in your document, ensure you are in Print Layout view. Comments will appear in the right margin.
   - To navigate between comments, click the Next or Previous buttons in the Comments group on the Review tab.

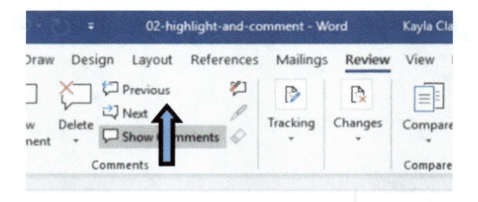

3. Replying to a Comment:
    - If you're collaborating with others, you can reply to comments. Click on an existing comment to select it, then click Reply in the comment box.
    - Your reply will appear under the original comment, creating a threaded conversation.

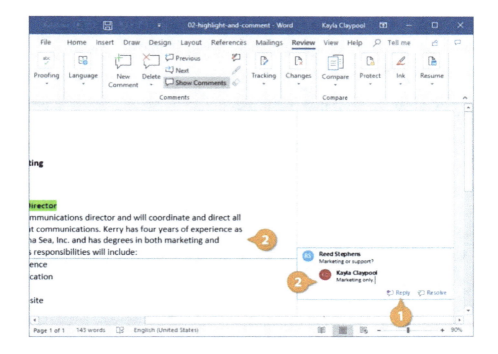

4. Deleting a Comment:
   o To delete a comment, right-click on the comment box and select Delete Comment. Alternatively, you can select the comment and press the Delete button in the Comments group on the Review tab.

Tip: Use comments to clarify doubts, suggest improvements, or provide additional context without altering the content of the document. This is especially helpful when collaborating on a document with multiple authors or reviewers.

Using Track Changes for Edits

Track Changes is a feature that allows you to make edits to a document while keeping a record of all changes. This feature is especially useful for document review and editing in collaborative projects, as it lets you see who made each change and easily accept or reject edits.

Step-by-Step Instructions:

1. Turning on Track Changes:
    o Go to the Review tab in the Ribbon.
    o In the Tracking group, click on Track Changes. The button will be highlighted when it's active.

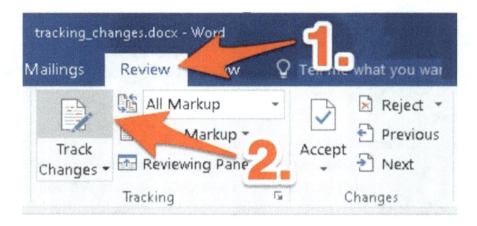

    o Once Track Changes is turned on, any edits you make to the document will be marked with a colored highlight or underline, and deletions will be shown with a strikethrough.

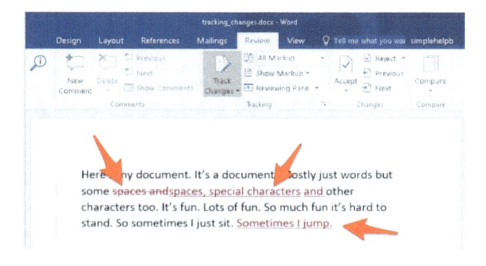

2. Making Edits with Track Changes:
    o   After Track Changes is activated, make any changes
        you need to the text. You'll notice that inserted text
        will appear in a different color, and deleted text will
        be crossed out.
    o   If you add or delete any content, the change will be
        visible to all collaborators.
3. Viewing Changes:
    o   You can choose how you view the tracked changes by
        clicking on the Display for Review dropdown in the
        Tracking group. You can select options such as All
        Markup, Simple Markup, or No Markup. The All
        Markup option shows every tracked change, while
        Simple Markup displays a cleaner version with only
        the final edits visible.
4. Accepting or Rejecting Changes:
    o   Once you or others have reviewed the changes, you
        can either accept or reject them.

- To accept or reject a change, right-click on the change and select Accept or Reject from the context menu. Alternatively, you can click Accept or Reject in the Changes group on the Review tab.
- To accept or reject all changes at once, click the dropdown arrow next to Accept or Reject, and select Accept All Changes or Reject All Changes.

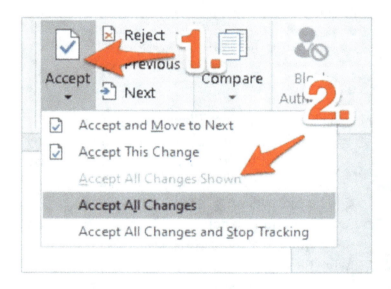

Tip: Track Changes helps maintain a transparent and organized review process, so everyone involved can easily see what edits have been made, who made them, and whether they were accepted or rejected.

Sharing a Document for Real-Time Collaboration

One of the best features of Microsoft Word is the ability to collaborate on a document in real-time. With cloud-based storage (OneDrive or SharePoint), multiple users can work on the same document simultaneously, making changes and adding comments without worrying about conflicting versions.

Step-by-Step Instructions:

1. Saving Your Document to OneDrive:
   - Before sharing a document for real-time collaboration, make sure it is saved to a cloud service like OneDrive.
   - To save to OneDrive, click on File, then Save As, and choose OneDrive as your location.
   - Name your document and click Save.

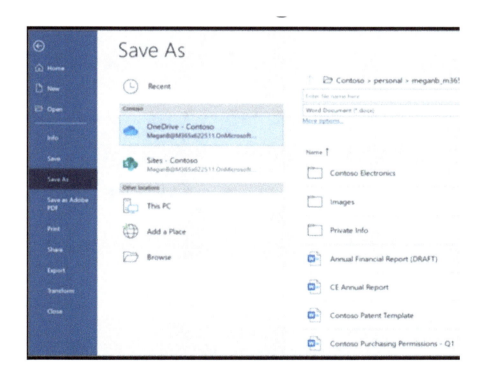

2. Sharing Your Document:
   - ○ Once the document is saved to OneDrive, go to the File tab.
   - ○ Click Share in the left menu.
   - ○ In the Share pane, you can either invite specific people by entering their email addresses or get a Shareable Link that you can send to anyone.
   - ○ You can choose whether collaborators can Edit or View the document.

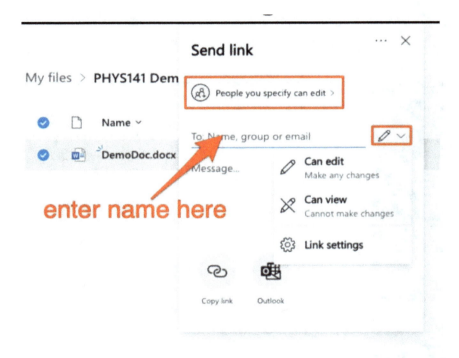

3. Collaborating in Real-Time:
   - ○ After sharing the document, anyone with the link (or those you invited) can open the document in Word or Word Online.

- You'll see who else is working on the document by looking at the small avatars or names in the top-right corner of the window.
- As people make changes, you'll see them in real-time. Changes will appear in different colors to indicate who made them.

4. Communicating in Real-Time:
   - Use the Comments feature to communicate with your collaborators in real-time. If you need clarification or want to ask a question, simply add a comment, and others will see it.
   - You can also use the @mention feature to tag specific people in comments or document text (e.g., @JohnDoe). This will send them a notification so they can respond promptly.

Tip: Real-time collaboration is perfect for team projects, joint reports, or any document where multiple people need to contribute or review at the same time. Just make sure you have a stable internet connection to take full advantage of this feature.

Summary: Working Smarter with Collaboration Tools

Microsoft Word's collaboration tools — including comments, Track Changes, and real-time sharing — make it easy to work together with others, whether you're writing, editing, or reviewing a document. By using these tools effectively, you can streamline your workflows, stay organized, and ensure that everyone's input is captured and addressed.

Chapter 15: Mail Merge

ail Merge is a powerful tool in Microsoft Word that allows you to create personalized documents for multiple recipients with just a few clicks. Whether you're sending out a bulk letter, creating custom labels, or printing envelopes, Mail Merge can save you valuable time and effort. This feature is particularly useful for businesses, organizations, or anyone who needs to send similar documents to many people, such as invitations, newsletters, or promotional materials.

In this chapter, we will walk through the essential steps to set up a Mail Merge, create labels and envelopes, and import data from other programs like Excel or Access. By the end of this chapter, you'll be able to create and personalize documents efficiently, enhancing your productivity.

Setting Up a Mail Merge for Letters

Mail Merge allows you to create a main document (like a letter) that is linked to a data source (such as a list of recipient names and addresses). This way, you can automatically personalize the content for each recipient in your list.

Step-by-Step Instructions:

1. Starting the Mail Merge:
   - Open a new or existing Word document.

- Go to the Mailings tab on the Ribbon.
- Click on Start Mail Merge, and select Letters from the dropdown. This indicates you're creating a letter and will allow you to connect to a data source (e.g., a list of recipients).

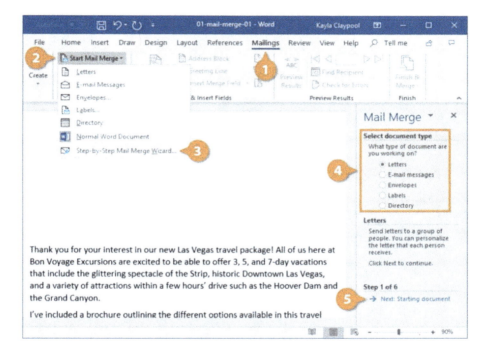

2. Choosing the Recipients:
- After selecting Letters, click Select Recipients in the Mail Merge group on the Mailings tab.
- Choose Use an Existing List if you already have a data source (such as an Excel file) with the names and addresses of your recipients.

o Browse to find the file you want to use and select it. The data from your file will now be available for use in your document.

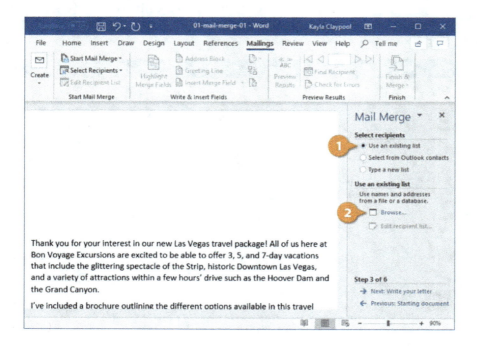

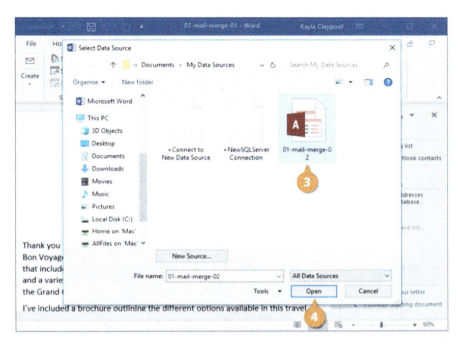

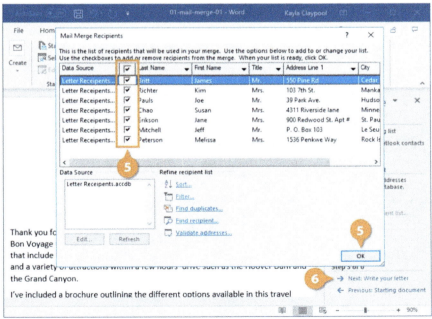

3. Inserting Merge Fields:

   o Place your cursor where you want the recipient's personalized information (like name or address) to appear in the document.

   o Click Insert Merge Field in the Mail Merge group, then select the field (e.g., First Name, Last Name, Address) that you want to insert.

   o The field will appear in your document as a placeholder, such as «First Name». This will be replaced by the actual information from your data source during the merge process.

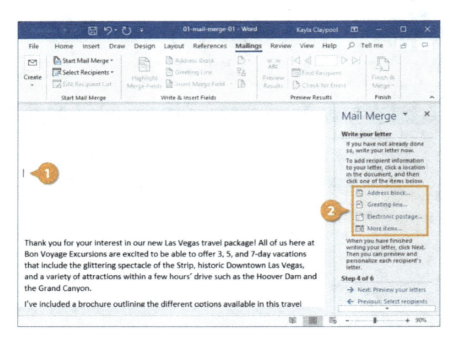

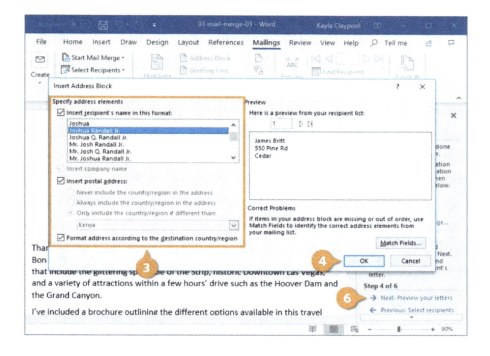

4. Previewing the Merge:
   o To see how the document will look for each recipient, click Preview Results in the Mail Merge group. This will show you how the placeholders are replaced with actual data.
   o Use the Next Record button to scroll through the merged documents and ensure everything looks correct.

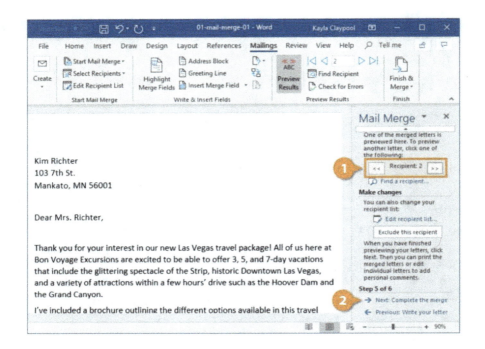

5. Completing the Mail Merge:
    o When you're satisfied with the preview, click Finish
      & Merge in the Mail Merge group.
    o Choose whether to Print Documents, Create a New
      Document, or Send Email Messages depending on
      your needs.
    o If you choose to create a new document, Word will
      generate a separate document with all the merged
      letters, each personalized for a different recipient.

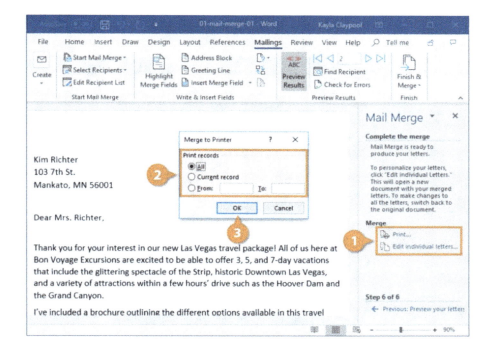

Tip: Make sure your data source is well-organized. For example, in Excel, your data should be set up with one column for each type of information (e.g., Name, Address, City) and each row representing a different recipient.

Creating Labels and Envelopes

Mail Merge isn't just for letters! You can also use it to create labels and envelopes for bulk mailings, saving you the time of manually entering each recipient's address.

Step-by-Step Instructions for Creating Labels:

1. Starting the Label Merge:
   o Go to the Mailings tab and click Start Mail Merge.

- Choose Labels from the dropdown.

- In the Label Options dialog box, select the type of labels you are using (e.g., Avery 5160). This will set the size and layout of the labels.

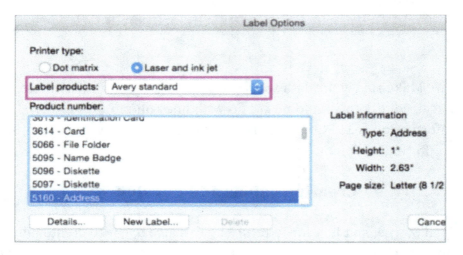

2. Selecting Recipients for the Labels:
    - Click Select Recipients, then choose Use an Existing List to import your recipient list from an Excel file or another data source.

- o After selecting your data source, choose the specific recipients you want to include in the merge.

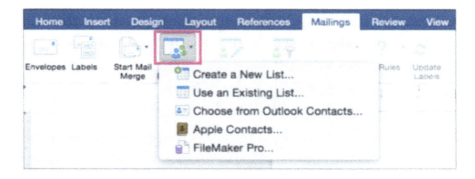

3. Inserting Merge Fields into the Label:
   - o Place your cursor in the first label.
   - o Click Insert Merge Field and choose the field(s) you want to appear on the label, such as Name, Address, City, etc.

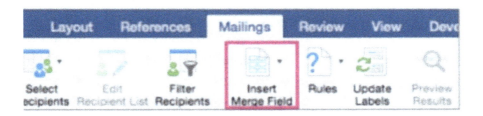

   - o After adding the fields, the label will look something like this: «First Name» «Last Name» on the first line, followed by the recipient's address.
4. Updating All Labels:
   - o After setting up the first label, click Update Labels in the Mail Merge group to apply the same layout to all the labels on the page.

- o This ensures that every label in your document will have the same design, pulling data from the appropriate fields.
5. Previewing and Printing:
   - o Click Preview Results to check how the labels will look with real data.
   - o When everything looks good, click Finish & Merge and select Print Documents to print your labels.

Step-by-Step Instructions for Creating Envelopes:

1. Starting the Envelope Merge:
   - o Go to the Mailings tab and click Start Mail Merge, then choose Envelopes.
   - o In the Envelope Options dialog box, select the envelope size you are using (e.g., #10 Envelope).
2. Selecting Recipients:
   - o Click Select Recipients, then choose Use an Existing List to import your recipient list.
   - o Select the data source (e.g., an Excel file) that contains the addresses for your envelopes.
3. Inserting the Address Fields:
   - o Click inside the envelope's layout area where you want the recipient's address to appear.
   - o Click Insert Merge Field and select the fields (e.g., Name, Address, City, State, Zip Code) you want to include.
   - o You can also add a return address by typing it manually or inserting a merge field for your own information.
4. Previewing and Printing:

- Click Preview Results to check how the addresses will appear on the envelopes.
- If everything looks correct, click Finish & Merge and select Print Documents to print your envelopes.

Tip: When creating labels or envelopes, double-check that the data fields are correctly aligned with the document layout. This ensures that everything fits properly on the label or envelope.

Importing Data from Excel or Access

To personalize your mail merge, you can import recipient data from external sources, such as Microsoft Excel or Access databases. This makes it easy to manage large mailing lists and update information as needed.

Step-by-Step Instructions for Importing Data from Excel:

1. Preparing Your Excel File:
   - In Excel, create a table with one column for each piece of information you want to include in the mail merge (e.g., First Name, Last Name, Address, etc.).
   - Make sure your data is organized with column headers at the top (e.g., First Name, Address), and each recipient's information is entered in a separate row.
2. Importing the Excel File into Word:
   - In Word, go to the Mailings tab and click Select Recipients.

- o Choose Use an Existing List and browse to find the Excel file containing your recipient data.
- o Select the file and choose the specific worksheet you want to use for the mail merge.
3. Mapping the Fields:
    - o Word will automatically match the column headers from your Excel file to the corresponding merge fields in your document.
    - o If necessary, you can manually match the Excel columns with the appropriate fields in your Word document by clicking Edit Recipient List.

Tip: When importing data from Excel or Access, always ensure your source data is clean and free from errors to avoid issues during the merge process. If your data is in multiple sheets in Excel, make sure to select the correct sheet during the import process.

Summary: Streamlining Your Document Creation with Mail Merge

Mail Merge is an essential tool for anyone who needs to send personalized documents to a large group of people. By using Mail Merge for letters, labels, and envelopes, you can save time and ensure consistency across all your documents. With the ability to import data from Excel or Access, you can easily manage your recipient lists and create custom documents that are tailored to each individual.

Part 6: Managing Your Work

Chapter 16: Printing and Exporting Documents

Microsoft Word allows you to produce professional-quality prints and easily export your documents into various formats. Whether you need to print a document for a meeting, share a finalized report with others, or save your work in PDF format for distribution, Word has tools that make this process straightforward. In this chapter, we'll guide you through the steps of printing your documents, adjusting print settings, and exporting your work to different file formats, including PDF.

Print Preview and Print Settings

Before printing a document, it's important to review how it will appear on paper. The Print Preview feature in Word helps you avoid costly printing errors and ensures that your document will look exactly as expected.

Step-by-Step Instructions:

1. Accessing Print Preview:
    o First, go to the File tab in the Ribbon.

- ○ Click on Print. This will open the Print Preview section, where you can see how the document will appear when printed.
- ○ In this view, you can navigate through each page of your document to ensure everything looks correct.
2. Navigating in Print Preview:
   - ○ Use the arrows on the right side to scroll through pages.
   - ○ If your document spans multiple pages, you can zoom in or out using the Zoom option at the bottom of the Print Preview window to get a closer look at the content.
   - ○ Review page breaks, headers, footers, and alignment.
3. Checking for Issues:
   - ○ In Print Preview, Word will display any issues such as content being cut off or misaligned.
   - ○ If something doesn't look right, exit Print Preview and make any necessary changes to your document's layout or formatting.
4. Selecting a Printer:
   - ○ In the Print section of the File tab, under Printer, select the printer you want to use from the dropdown list. If you are printing to a PDF or another file format, this will be your selected output destination.
5. Adjusting the Number of Copies:

- o In the Copies field, specify how many copies of the document you need to print.
- o Word will automatically print the number of copies you specify, which is helpful for bulk printing.

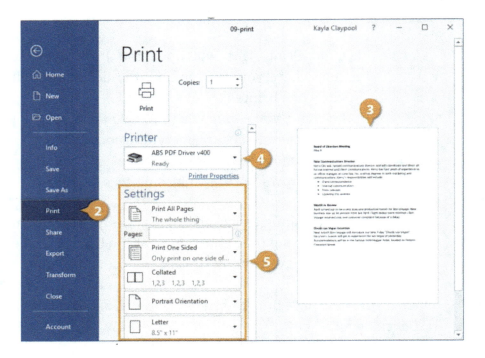

Tip: Always perform a print preview to ensure there are no issues with the layout before sending it to the printer. This can save paper and time, especially when printing long documents.

Selecting Paper Size and Layout

Microsoft Word offers various options for customizing the size and layout of your printed document. You can change the paper size, orientation (portrait or landscape), and other settings to meet your specific needs.

Step-by-Step Instructions:

1. Choosing Paper Size:
   - In the Print section of the File tab, click Printer Properties (this may vary depending on your printer).
   - Alternatively, go to the Layout tab on the Ribbon and click Size to select from standard sizes like Letter, Legal, or A4. You can also choose Custom Size if your printer supports non-standard sizes.
2. Setting Page Orientation:
   - To change the orientation (portrait or landscape), go to the Layout tab.
   - In the Page Setup group, click Orientation and choose either Portrait (vertical) or Landscape (horizontal).
   - This is particularly useful if you are printing wide tables or graphics that need extra horizontal space.
3. Adjusting Margins:
   - In the Layout tab, click on Margins and select from predefined margin options (e.g., Normal, Narrow, Wide).
   - For customized margins, select Custom Margins at the bottom of the list, where you can manually enter the top, bottom, left, and right margins.
4. Scaling Your Document:
   - If your content doesn't fit well on the page, you can use the Scale to Paper Size feature in the Print Preview.

- Click Fit to in the print settings and select the desired paper size. Word will automatically resize your document to fit on that size paper.

Tip: Always double-check the page layout before printing. If you're using a custom paper size, make sure your printer supports it to avoid printing errors.

Exporting to PDF and Other Formats

In addition to printing, Microsoft Word allows you to export your document to different formats, making it easy to share and store your work. PDF is one of the most common formats for distributing documents that you don't want to be edited. Word also supports exporting to formats such as HTML, plain text (TXT), and more.

Step-by-Step Instructions:

1. Exporting to PDF:
   - Go to the File tab and click on Export.
   - Select Create PDF/XPS Document. This will open the Publish as PDF or XPS dialog box.
   - Choose the location where you want to save your PDF, enter a file name, and click Publish.
   - You can adjust additional options by clicking Options in the dialog box, where you can choose to export the entire document or just specific pages, among other settings.
2. Saving as Other File Formats:
   - In the File tab, click on Save As.

- o Choose the location to save your document, then select Save as Type from the dropdown list.
- o In addition to PDF, you can save your document in various formats, such as:
  - Word Document (.docx) – Standard Word format.
  - Word 97-2003 Document (.doc) – Older Word formats.
  - Plain Text (.txt) – No formatting, only text.
  - HTML (.html) – Export as a webpage.
  - RTF (.rtf) – Rich Text Format, which can be opened by many word processors.
3. Sending Documents via Email:
   - o You can also send your document directly via email without leaving Word.
   - o In the File tab, click Share and select Email.
   - o Choose to send the document as an attachment, or you can select Send as PDF to attach the file in PDF format.
4. Using Word to Create a PDF Portfolio:
   - o If you have multiple Word documents or files you want to bundle together into a single PDF, use the Create PDF/XPS Document option.
   - o Combine multiple Word files into a single document by copying and pasting or using the Insert tab to insert other Word documents.

Tip: When exporting to PDF, make sure to check your document formatting one last time in Print Preview. Sometimes, converting to PDF can alter spacing or layout slightly, so you want to ensure that the final version looks as expected.

Summary: Printing and Exporting Documents

In this chapter, we covered the essential steps for printing and exporting documents from Microsoft Word. By using the Print Preview feature, you can ensure that your document looks perfect before you print it, saving you from making costly mistakes. Selecting the right paper size, orientation, and layout will help you achieve the desired appearance. Additionally, exporting your work to formats like PDF gives you the flexibility to share your documents digitally, without worrying about unintentional edits. Whether printing a letter or sending a report, Microsoft Word makes the process straightforward and efficient.

Chapter 17: Document Security

When working with documents in Microsoft Word, especially when they contain sensitive or confidential information, it's essential to protect your files from unauthorized access or accidental edits. Microsoft Word offers a variety of security features that allow you to safeguard your documents, whether you're sharing them online or working with others. In this chapter, we'll walk through how to apply password protection, restrict editing, and inspect documents for sensitive data to ensure your work remains secure.

Protecting Your Document with Passwords

Adding a password to your Word document is a powerful way to ensure that only authorized people can access your content. Whether you're sharing a sensitive report, personal information, or business documents, a password will prevent unauthorized users from opening the file.

Step-by-Step Instructions:

1. Opening the Document You Want to Protect:
   o Launch Microsoft Word and open the document you want to secure.
2. Setting a Password:
   o Click on the File tab in the Ribbon to open the backstage view.

- In the Info section, click Protect Document.
- From the drop-down menu, select Encrypt with Password.

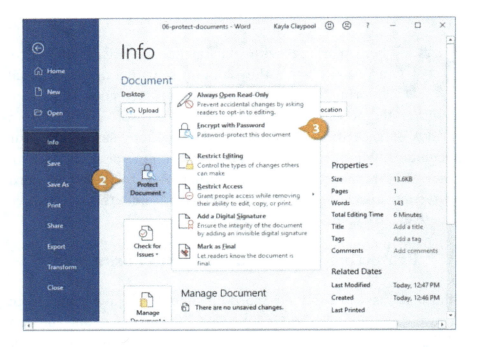

- A dialog box will appear, prompting you to enter a password. Type a strong password, and then re-enter it to confirm.
  - Tip: Choose a password that's long, includes a mix of uppercase and lowercase letters, numbers, and special characters to make it harder to guess.
- Click OK to apply the password.

3. Saving Your Document with the Password:
   o   After setting the password, save the document. Now, every time someone tries to open the document, they will be prompted to enter the password.
   o   Keep the password secure and avoid sharing it with unauthorized individuals.
4. Removing a Password:
   o   To remove a password, repeat the steps to open the Encrypt with Password dialog box.
   o   Delete the existing password, and click OK to save the document without encryption.

Important Consideration: If you forget the password, there is no easy way to recover the document. Always store the password securely.

Restricting Editing for Shared Files

When working on documents with others, you may want to limit the changes they can make. Word offers the ability to restrict editing permissions, allowing you to control who can make edits and what they can edit.

Step-by-Step Instructions:

1. Opening the Document for Editing Restriction:
   o   Open the document you want to restrict editing for.
2. Enabling Editing Restrictions:
   o   Click on the File tab and select Info.

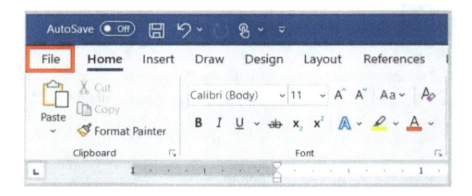

o Choose Protect Document, then select Restrict Editing.

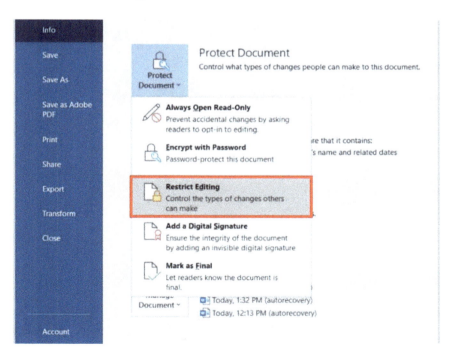

- A panel will appear on the right side of the window, where you can set the restrictions.
3. Setting Editing Restrictions:
    - In the Restrict Editing panel, under the Editing Restrictions section, check the box for Allow only this type of editing in the document.
    - From the drop-down menu, you can choose:
        - No changes (Read only): The document is view-only and cannot be edited.
        - Comments: Users can only add comments, but not edit the main text.
        - Filling in forms: Users can only fill out forms if the document has form fields.
    - Additionally, you can choose to allow users to track changes, making it easier to review edits.

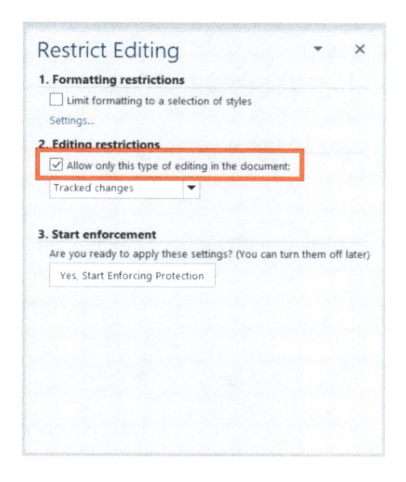

4. Password-Protecting the Editing Restrictions:
    o To ensure that only authorized users can remove the editing restrictions, click on Yes, Start Enforcing Protection at the bottom of the panel.

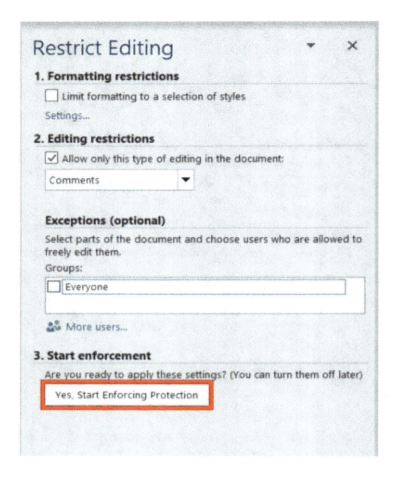

- o Enter a password in the pop-up box and click OK. This will prevent others from easily changing the restrictions you've set.

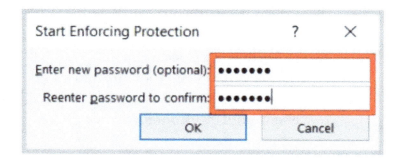

5. Saving the Restricted Document:
    o Once the restrictions are set, save the document. Now, users who open the document will be subject to the limitations you've defined, whether it's read-only access or restricted editing.

Tip: You can also restrict specific sections of a document. For instance, you might want to allow changes to only one part of a report while locking the rest of the document. To do this, you can use the Sections feature to apply restrictions to individual parts.

Inspecting Documents for Sensitive Information

When sharing documents, especially with external parties, it's important to ensure that no sensitive information remains in the file. Microsoft Word provides a feature called Document Inspector, which helps you find and remove hidden data like personal information, comments, tracked changes, or even document properties that you may not want to share.

Step-by-Step Instructions:

1. Opening the Document to Inspect:

- Open the document you want to inspect for hidden information.
2. Accessing the Document Inspector:
   - Click on the File tab and go to the Info section.
   - Click on Check for Issues, then select Inspect Document from the drop-down menu.

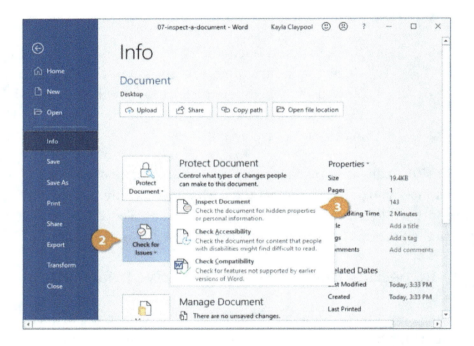

3. Running the Document Inspector:
   - In the Document Inspector window, select the types of information you want to check for. You can choose to inspect the following:
     - Comments, revisions, and annotations: This includes all comments and tracked changes in the document.

- Document properties and personal information: This includes author names, company names, and any other metadata embedded in the file.
- Headers, footers, and footnotes: Ensure there's no hidden data in these areas.
- Hidden text: Sometimes, text is formatted as hidden, which could be inadvertently included in the document.

4. Reviewing and Removing Sensitive Information:
   - After selecting what to inspect, click Inspect.

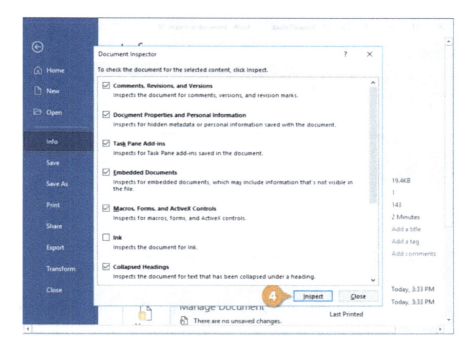

   - Word will display a list of the findings, showing you any hidden information. You can choose to remove

the unwanted data by clicking Remove All next to
each type of hidden information.

○ Once you've removed any sensitive information, click
Close.

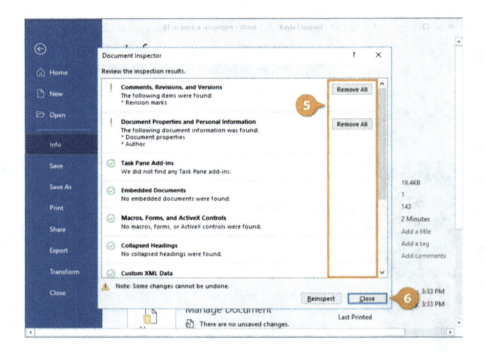

5. Saving the Clean Document:

○ After cleaning up the document, save it to ensure that
the document is now free of any sensitive data.

Important Consideration: Always run the Document Inspector
before sharing documents, especially when dealing with legal,
financial, or personal information. Hidden metadata can often be
overlooked, leading to potential privacy or security risks.

Summary: Document Security

In this chapter, we've covered important steps to secure your documents in Microsoft Word. By setting passwords, restricting editing, and inspecting your document for sensitive information, you can protect your files from unauthorized access, accidental changes, or unintentional leaks of private data.

Microsoft Word provides powerful tools to ensure that only the right people can view or modify your work. As you move forward, always consider the security of your documents, especially when sharing them with others.

Part 7: Troubleshooting and Tips

Chapter 18: Common Problems and Solutions

E ven with Microsoft Word's powerful tools and user-friendly interface, it's not uncommon to run into a few bumps along the way. Whether it's formatting issues, unexpected alignment problems, or a document that unexpectedly disappears or becomes corrupted, every Word user, from beginners to experienced ones, can face challenges. Fortunately, Microsoft Word has built-in features to help you solve these common problems. In this chapter, we'll discuss solutions to some of the most common issues you might encounter while using Word.

Resolving Formatting Issues

Formatting inconsistencies can happen for several reasons: accidental keystrokes, importing text from another document, or even copying content from the web. These issues often result in inconsistent fonts, spacing, or overall layout problems. Let's go through a few of the most common formatting issues and how to fix them.

Step-by-Step Instructions:

1. Fixing Inconsistent Fonts or Sizes:
    o   Use the Format Painter Tool:

- If part of your document looks different in terms of font, size, or color, you can use the Format Painter tool to apply the correct formatting across multiple areas of text.
- To use it:
  - Highlight the correctly formatted text.
  - Go to the Home tab in the Ribbon and click on the Format Painter (the paintbrush icon).
  - Now, drag your mouse across the text you want to reformat. The same font and formatting will be applied to it.

2. Removing Unwanted Formatting (Clear All Formatting):
   - If your text has unwanted formatting, you can clear it.
   - Highlight the affected text and go to the Home tab.
   - In the Font group, click Clear All Formatting (the eraser icon). This will remove bold, italics, font size changes, colors, and more, reverting your text to the default style.

3. Using Styles for Consistent Formatting:
   - One of the best ways to ensure consistent formatting throughout your document is to use Styles. These are pre-defined formatting options for headings, body text, and other parts of your document.
   - To apply a style:
     - Highlight the text you want to format.
     - In the Home tab, go to the Styles group and choose a style (Heading 1, Normal, etc.).
     - If you don't see the style you want, you can customize the styles by right-clicking on the style name and choosing Modify.

4. Handling Section Breaks and Formatting:
   - Sometimes, formatting issues arise from section breaks or page breaks. To remove or modify section breaks:
     - Go to the View tab and select Draft view.
     - Scroll through the document to locate section breaks. They are often marked as "Section Break (Next Page)" or "Continuous."
     - Place your cursor before the break and press Delete to remove it, or modify it to suit your layout needs.

Fixing Alignment and Spacing Problems

Misaligned text and irregular spacing are common complaints that many users face. These issues often happen when text has been copied from another source, when paragraph settings are inconsistent, or when margins and alignment are not set correctly.

Step-by-Step Instructions:

1. Aligning Text (Left, Center, Right, Justify):
   - To fix alignment issues, select the text that is misaligned.
   - In the Home tab, in the Paragraph group, you will find alignment buttons:
     - Left Align (Ctrl + L) aligns the text to the left.
     - Center Align (Ctrl + E) centers the text.
     - Right Align (Ctrl + R) aligns the text to the right.

- Justify (Ctrl + J) spreads the text evenly between the left and right margins.
2. Fixing Line and Paragraph Spacing:
   - Sometimes, too much or too little space between lines or paragraphs can make your document look disorganized.
   - To adjust line spacing:
     - Highlight the text you want to adjust.
     - In the Home tab, in the Paragraph group, click on the Line and Paragraph Spacing button (the up-and-down arrows icon).
     - Choose the desired line spacing (e.g., 1.0, 1.5, 2.0).
     - To customize further, click on Line Spacing Options at the bottom of the dropdown menu and adjust settings like Before and After spacing.
3. Removing Extra Spacing Between Paragraphs:
   - Microsoft Word sometimes adds additional space between paragraphs automatically.
   - To remove it:
     - Go to the Home tab, click the Paragraph settings dialog box launcher (small arrow in the corner of the Paragraph group).
     - In the Spacing section, set both Before and After to 0 pt, and ensure Line Spacing is set to Single.
4. Fixing Indentation Issues:
   - Indentation problems can make text look off-center or inconsistent. To adjust indentations:
     - Highlight the paragraph(s) you want to adjust.

- In the Home tab, click the Increase Indent or Decrease Indent button.
- For more advanced indentation settings, click the Paragraph Settings dialog box launcher and modify the Indentation section under Special (First Line, Hanging, or None).

5. Clearing Extra Spaces:
   - Sometimes, extra spaces or invisible characters like tabs or extra paragraph marks appear in a document.
   - To reveal these characters, go to the Home tab, and click on the Show/Hide ¶ button in the Paragraph group. This will display spaces, tabs, and paragraph markers that can be deleted.

Recovering Lost or Corrupted Files

It's every Word user's worst nightmare: working for hours on a document only to lose it due to a system crash, power failure, or accidental deletion. Fortunately, Word offers several ways to recover lost or corrupted files.

Step-by-Step Instructions:

1. AutoRecover:
   - Microsoft Word automatically saves temporary versions of your documents every few minutes.
   - To recover a document that was not saved:
     - Open Microsoft Word and click on File.
     - Select Info and look under Manage Document.
     - Choose Recover Unsaved Documents. You will see a list of unsaved files that Word has stored.

Select the file you want to recover and click Open.

- Save the recovered document immediately.

2. Using Previous Versions:
   o If a document has become corrupted or accidentally deleted, you may be able to restore a previous version.
   o Right-click on the document in File Explorer and choose Restore previous versions. A list of available versions will appear, allowing you to select a version to restore.

3. Repairing Corrupted Files:
   o In the event of a corrupted document, Word may not open the file at all. If this happens, try to open it using Word's Open and Repair feature:
     - Open Word, go to File, then click on Open.
     - Browse to the corrupted document, select it, and click the down arrow next to the Open button.
     - Choose Open and Repair. Word will attempt to fix the document and open it.

4. Recovering Files from Cloud Storage:
   o If you've been saving your documents to a cloud service like OneDrive or SharePoint, you may be able to recover an earlier version directly from the cloud.
   o Go to the cloud service's website, locate the file, and check for version history options to restore a previous version.

Summary: Common Problems and Solutions

In this chapter, we've covered some of the most common problems Word users encounter, and we've provided you with step-by-step instructions to solve these issues. Whether it's dealing with formatting inconsistencies, alignment and spacing problems, or recovering a lost document, Microsoft Word offers a variety of tools to help you maintain a smooth workflow.

Remember, these tools are here to make your experience more efficient, but sometimes the simplest problems can be the trickiest to fix. Don't be afraid to use the built-in help functions and the vast array of tutorials and online resources that Microsoft provides.

Chapter 19: Time-Saving Tips

W orking with Microsoft Word is all about efficiency—getting your tasks done faster, with less effort. This chapter is designed to help you boost your productivity by mastering a few key time-saving tools and tricks that can save you hours in the long run. From keyboard shortcuts to automating repetitive tasks with macros, these tips will make your Word experience smoother and faster.

Using Keyboard Shortcuts

Keyboard shortcuts are one of the most effective ways to speed up your work in Word. By memorizing just a few key combinations, you can perform common tasks in a fraction of the time it would take to navigate the menus and ribbons. Here's how to master keyboard shortcuts for common actions:

Step-by-Step Instructions:

1. Essential Keyboard Shortcuts:
   - Ctrl + N – Create a new document.
   - Ctrl + O – Open an existing document.
   - Ctrl + S – Save the current document.
   - Ctrl + P – Open the Print dialog box.
   - Ctrl + C – Copy selected text or object.
   - Ctrl + X – Cut selected text or object.
   - Ctrl + V – Paste copied or cut content.

- Ctrl + Z – Undo the last action.
- Ctrl + Y – Redo the last undone action.
- Ctrl + A – Select all content in the document.
- Ctrl + B – Bold the selected text.
- Ctrl + I – Italicize the selected text.
- Ctrl + U – Underline the selected text.
- Ctrl + F – Open the Find feature to search within the document.
- Ctrl + H – Open the Find and Replace dialog box.

2. Using the Function Keys: Function keys (F1 through F12) also have specific shortcuts in Word that can save you time.
   - F1 – Opens Word Help.
   - F7 – Opens the spelling and grammar checker.
   - Ctrl + F12 – Opens the "Open" dialog box to select a file to open.
   - F12 – Saves the document as a new file (Save As).

3. Learn the Common Shortcut Combinations:
   - Ctrl + Shift + L – Apply the bulleted list style.
   - Ctrl + E – Center align the text.
   - Ctrl + R – Right align the text.
   - Ctrl + J – Justify the text (aligns both left and right).
   - Ctrl + M – Indent the selected paragraph.
   - Ctrl + T – Remove hanging indent.

4. Navigating With Shortcuts:
   - Ctrl + Arrow keys – Move the cursor word by word rather than character by character.
   - Ctrl + Shift + Arrow keys – Select text by word rather than by letter.
   - Home – Move the cursor to the beginning of the line.
   - End – Move the cursor to the end of the line.

- Ctrl + Home – Move the cursor to the beginning of the document.
- Ctrl + End – Move the cursor to the end of the document.

By learning these essential keyboard shortcuts, you'll cut down on the time spent clicking through menus, making your workflow much more efficient.

Customizing the Quick Access Toolbar

The Quick Access Toolbar (QAT) in Microsoft Word is a handy feature that allows you to add your most frequently used commands, providing you with one-click access to tools you use all the time. Customizing this toolbar to suit your needs will save you from having to dig through tabs or the Ribbon to find the right commands.

Step-by-Step Instructions:

1. Adding Commands to the Quick Access Toolbar:
   - Open Microsoft Word and look for the Quick Access Toolbar at the top-left corner of the window (above the Ribbon).
   - Click the downward arrow at the end of the toolbar.
   - A dropdown menu will appear with a list of common commands like Save, Undo, Redo, etc.
   - To add a command, simply click on it. It will immediately be added to the toolbar.
2. Adding More Commands:

- o If you need a command that isn't listed in the dropdown menu:
  - Click More Commands from the dropdown menu.
  - In the Word Options window, you'll see a list of available commands.
  - Select the command you want to add, click Add, and then click OK. It will appear in your Quick Access Toolbar.
  - Common examples of commands to add: Bold, Copy, Paste, Spelling & Grammar, Print Preview, etc.
3. Reordering Quick Access Toolbar Items:
   - o To change the order of commands on the Quick Access Toolbar, click the downward arrow again and choose More Commands.
   - o In the Word Options window, select a command and use the Up or Down arrows to change its position.
   - o Click OK to save the changes.
4. Removing Commands:
   - o If you no longer need a command on the Quick Access Toolbar, click the downward arrow and uncheck the command you want to remove.
5. Using the Toolbar for Even More Efficiency:
   - o Pinning Items to the Toolbar: If you use a command that's hidden within the Ribbon, you can pin it to the Quick Access Toolbar for faster access.
   - o Right-clicking for Quick Access: Right-click on any command or button on the Ribbon, and choose Add to Quick Access Toolbar.

Customizing the Quick Access Toolbar ensures that your most-used features are right at your fingertips, making your workflow more efficient and personalized.

Creating Macros for Repetitive Tasks

For tasks you perform regularly, macros can be a huge time-saver. A macro is a small program you can create in Word that automates a series of actions. Instead of repeating the same steps over and over, a macro lets you perform them all with a single command. Let's take a closer look at how to set up and use macros in Word.

Step-by-Step Instructions:

1. What is a Macro?
   - A macro is a sequence of commands and instructions that you group together to accomplish a task automatically. For example, if you frequently insert a certain header, apply a specific formatting style, and add a date, a macro can do all that in one go.
2. Recording a Macro:
   - Go to the View tab in the Ribbon and click Macros, then select Record Macro.
   - You will be prompted to give the macro a name and a shortcut key. (For example, you could name it "InsertHeader" and assign it Ctrl + Shift + H for easy access.)
   - Choose where you want to store the macro:
     - All Documents (Normal.dotm) – Available for all documents you create in Word.

- This Document – Available only in the current document.
  - o Once you click OK, Word will start recording your actions.
  - o Perform the series of actions you want to automate (e.g., formatting a paragraph, adding a specific image).
  - o When you're done, click View > Macros > Stop Recording.
3. Running the Macro:
   - o To run the macro you've just created, either use the keyboard shortcut you assigned or go to View > Macros > View Macros.
   - o In the Macros dialog box, select your macro and click Run.
4. Editing a Macro:
   - o If you want to edit your macro, go to View > Macros > View Macros, select the macro, and click Edit.
   - o This will open the Visual Basic for Applications (VBA) editor, where you can adjust the code that runs your macro.
   - o You can also record a new macro if you need to tweak the original one further.
5. Assigning Macros to Buttons or Keys:
   - o You can assign your macro to a button or a keyboard shortcut for even quicker access.
   - o To do this, go to File > Options > Customize Ribbon or Quick Access Toolbar.
   - o Choose Macros from the dropdown list, select the macro, and click Add to place it in the Ribbon or toolbar.

- For a keyboard shortcut, go to File > Options > Customize Ribbon, then click Keyboard shortcuts at the bottom and assign the shortcut to your macro.
6. Managing Macros:
   - To delete a macro, go to View > Macros > View Macros, select the macro, and click Delete.

Summary: Time-Saving Tips

By incorporating these time-saving tips into your Microsoft Word routine, you'll be able to work much more efficiently. Whether it's using keyboard shortcuts, customizing your Quick Access Toolbar, or automating repetitive tasks with macros, these techniques will allow you to focus on what matters—creating high-quality documents with ease.

Part 8: Appendices

Chapter 20: Practice Exercises

To truly master Microsoft Word, practice is key. This chapter provides a set of beginner-level exercises designed to help reinforce the concepts and techniques you've learned in the previous chapters. These exercises include tasks like creating a resume and designing a newsletter, which will give you hands-on experience working with Word in practical situations. By completing these exercises, you'll solidify your skills and feel more confident using Word for everyday tasks.

Beginner-Level Tasks to Reinforce Learning

These beginner exercises are designed to help you put into practice the fundamental skills you've learned. These tasks will guide you through key Word features and help you get comfortable using them.

Exercise 1: Basic Text Formatting

1. Create a new blank document.
2. Type the following text:
   "Microsoft Word is a powerful word processing software. It helps you create and edit documents with ease."
3. Select the text and apply the following formatting:
   - o Change the font to Arial.
   - o Set the font size to 14.
   - o Apply bold and italic to the word "powerful".

- o   Underline the word "edit".
4. Change the font color of the entire sentence to blue.
5. Highlight the word "ease" and apply a yellow highlight.

Exercise 2: Paragraph Formatting

1. Create a new paragraph with the following text:
   "This is an example paragraph to practice alignment, indentation, and spacing. You will also create a list here."
2. Align the text to the center.
3. Indent the first line of the paragraph by 0.5 inches.
4. Add space before and after the paragraph by setting the paragraph spacing to 6 pt.
5. Create a bulleted list with the following items:
   - o   Apples
   - o   Bananas
   - o   Grapes
6. Change the list style to a numbered list.
7. Change the alignment of the text to justified.

Exercise 3: Inserting and Formatting Visual Elements

1. Open a new document and type:
   "Inserting images makes documents more visually appealing."
2. Insert an image of your choice from the web or your computer.
3. Resize the image to fit neatly within the text by dragging its corners.
4. Use text wrapping to make the text wrap around the image. Choose Square text wrapping.

5. Insert a shape (e.g., a rectangle) below the image and add some text inside the shape.

Sample Projects

These sample projects are designed to give you practical experience with common types of documents that you might create in Word, like resumes and newsletters.

Project 1: Creating a Resume

1. Open a new document and save it as "My Resume".
2. Type your name at the top of the page and apply the following formatting:
   - Set the font size to 18.
   - Make the name bold and centered on the page.
3. Below your name, create the following sections:
   - Contact Information (Name, Address, Phone Number, Email)
   - Objective Statement (A brief sentence stating your career goal)
   - Skills (List 3-5 relevant skills using a bulleted list)
   - Experience (List any relevant work experience or internships in chronological order)
   - Education (List your degree(s), school(s), and graduation year(s))
4. Use headings to format the section titles.
5. Add page numbers in the footer.
6. Save and review your resume to make sure it looks neat and professional.

Project 2: Creating a Newsletter

1. Open a new document and save it as "Company Newsletter".
2. At the top, create a header that includes your company's name and logo (if applicable).
3. Below the header, create a main article with the title "This Month's News" and write a short paragraph summarizing your company's latest updates.
4. Add a section for upcoming events:
   - List 3-4 upcoming events, each with a title, date, and brief description. Use a bulleted list.
5. Insert an image that complements your article.
6. Create a footer with the following:
   - Contact information
   - Social media handles (use hyperlinks)
7. Save and print the newsletter to see how it looks in hard copy format.

Review and Practice

Once you've completed these exercises and projects, take a moment to review what you've learned. Try to apply these skills to real-life scenarios such as creating reports, drafting emails, or designing presentations. The more you practice, the more comfortable you'll become with using Microsoft Word.

As you gain more experience, continue to challenge yourself with more advanced tasks. Word has many powerful features that you can explore, and with each new feature, you'll be able to work more efficiently and creatively.

By practicing these tasks and projects, you're building a solid foundation for using Microsoft Word confidently and effectively.

Summary

This chapter's practice exercises and sample projects provide you with the opportunity to apply the skills you've learned throughout the book. Whether it's formatting text, creating documents like resumes and newsletters, or working with visual elements, these exercises will help you become proficient in using Microsoft Word. Practice regularly to reinforce your skills and build confidence.

Chapter 21: Glossary of Terms

I n this chapter, we'll provide clear definitions of the most common Microsoft Word terms to help you understand the vocabulary and features used throughout the program. Familiarizing yourself with these terms will enhance your proficiency in navigating and using Word effectively. Whether you're reading this book or exploring the program on your own, knowing the meaning of these terms is essential to mastering Microsoft Word.

A

Alignment
The positioning of text in relation to the page or margin (left, center, right, or justified).

AutoCorrect
A feature in Microsoft Word that automatically corrects common spelling, typing, or formatting errors as you type.

AutoSave
A feature that automatically saves your document at regular intervals to prevent data loss.

B

Bullet Points
A type of list format that uses symbols (usually dots) at the start of each line to separate items in a list.

Bookmark
A tool in Word used to mark a location or section of text so you can easily navigate back to it.

Borders
Lines that are added around paragraphs, pages, or sections for visual emphasis.

C

Carriage Return
The act of pressing the Enter key to create a new line or paragraph in a document.

Clipboard
A temporary storage area in your computer's memory where text or images are stored after being cut or copied, ready to be pasted elsewhere.

Comments
Annotations or notes that can be added to a document to provide feedback or additional information without altering the content.

D

Document
A file created in Microsoft Word containing text, graphics, and other content.

Drag and Drop
A technique used to move text, images, or files by selecting the item, holding down the mouse button, dragging it to a new location, and releasing the mouse button.

Dropdown Menu
A list of options that appears when you click on a menu or button in the ribbon or toolbar.

E

Endnotes
Text at the end of a document that provides additional information or citations, often used in academic writing.

Equations
Mathematical formulas that can be inserted into a Word document using the built-in equation editor.

F

Font
The style, size, and appearance of text characters in a document.

Footer
The section at the bottom of each page in a Word document, where you can add elements like page numbers or document titles.

Formatting
The process of changing the appearance of text and objects in a document, such as font style, size, color, and alignment.

Find and Replace
A feature that allows you to search for specific words or phrases in a document and replace them with others.

G

Go To
A feature that allows you to quickly navigate to a specific page, section, or element within a document.

Graphics
Visual elements like images, charts, shapes, or diagrams that can be inserted into a Word document.

H

Header
The section at the top of each page in a document, where you can insert page numbers, document title, or other information.

Hyperlink
A clickable link that takes you to a different location in the document, another document, or a webpage.

I

Indentation
The space between the text and the left or right margin, often used to signal the start of a new paragraph.

Insert Tab
The tab in the ribbon that gives you access to a variety of insert options like images, tables, shapes, and links.

Interactive Content
Elements in a document, such as forms or hyperlinks, that allow the reader to interact with the content.

J

Justify
Text alignment where the text is spaced out to ensure that both the left and right edges of the paragraph align with the margins.

K

Keyboard Shortcuts
Predefined combinations of keyboard keys used to quickly
perform tasks, such as Ctrl+C for copy or Ctrl+P for print.

L

Layout
The arrangement and formatting of elements on the page, including
text, images, and other objects.

Line Spacing
The amount of space between lines of text in a paragraph.
Common options include single, 1.5, and double spacing.

M

Mail Merge
A feature that allows you to create personalized documents (e.g.,
letters, labels) by combining a Word document with a data source
like an Excel file.

Margins
The blank space around the edges of the page that defines the
printable area.

Macro
A sequence of actions that can be recorded and saved to automate repetitive tasks in Word.

N

Navigation Pane
A feature that allows you to quickly find and navigate through headings, pages, or sections within a Word document.

Numbered List
A list format that uses numbers or letters to organize items sequentially.

O

Office Clipboard
A clipboard specifically used in Microsoft Office applications to temporarily store up to 24 items for copying and pasting.

Orientation
The direction in which a document is printed: Portrait (vertical) or Landscape (horizontal).

P

Page Break
A manual break inserted into the document to end one page and start another.

Paragraph Styles
Predefined formats for paragraphs that can include font, spacing, alignment, and other settings, making it easy to apply consistent formatting.

Paste
A command that allows you to insert previously copied or cut content into a new location.

Q

Quick Access Toolbar
A customizable toolbar located above or below the ribbon that provides easy access to frequently used commands.

R

Ribbon
The toolbar at the top of the Word window, divided into tabs, that provides access to various commands and features.

Ruler
A tool used to measure and adjust margins, tab stops, and indents in your document.

Redline
The display of tracked changes in a document, often shown in red, indicating edits and revisions.

S

Search
A feature that allows you to find specific words or phrases within a document.

Section Break
A break used to divide a document into sections, allowing different formatting for each section.

SmartArt
Pre-designed graphics used to visually represent information, such as process flows or organizational charts.

T

Tab Stops
Locations on the ruler that define where text or objects will be aligned when you press the Tab key.

Table
A grid of rows and columns used to organize information within a Word document.

Track Changes
A feature that allows edits and revisions to be marked in a document, enabling you to review changes made by others.

U

Underline
A text formatting option that places a line beneath selected text.

Undo
A command used to reverse the last action you performed.

V

View Modes
Different ways to view and navigate your document, including Print Layout, Web Layout, and Read Mode.

Version History
A feature that tracks and stores previous versions of a document, allowing you to view or restore older versions.

W

Word Count
A tool that shows the total number of words, characters, and paragraphs in a document.

Watermark
A faint image or text placed in the background of a document, often used for security purposes (e.g., "Confidential").

X

XML
Extensible Markup Language, used for structuring data within documents.

Y

Y-axis
The vertical axis in a graph or chart.

Z

Zoom
A feature that allows you to change the magnification of the document to view content more closely or broadly.

Summary

This glossary of terms provides you with definitions for key Microsoft Word terminology, which will help you become more comfortable navigating and using the software. Understanding these terms is essential for getting the most out of Word's features and tools. As you continue to use Word, you'll become more familiar with these concepts, and they'll help you communicate more effectively when discussing or troubleshooting your documents.

Chapter 22: FAQs (Frequently Asked Questions)

In this chapter, we'll address some of the most commonly asked questions by beginners who are just starting to explore Microsoft Word. Whether you're dealing with basic setup issues, formatting challenges, or figuring out how to make the most of advanced features, this section is designed to provide clear and concise solutions to common problems. Let's dive into some of the frequently asked questions.

How do I start a new document in Microsoft Word?

To start a new document, follow these steps:

1. Open Microsoft Word: Click on the Word icon to launch the application.
2. Create a Blank Document: On the homepage, you can either select "Blank Document" or press Ctrl+N to create a new document.
3. Choose a Template: If you want a pre-designed layout, click on "New" and choose a template from the available options.

Starting from scratch or using a template depends on your needs, but both are equally simple.

How can I save my document?

To save your document:

1. Click on "File" in the top-left corner of the screen.
2. Select "Save" (or press Ctrl+S) if this is your first time saving the document.
3. Choose the location on your computer where you want to save the file, and give it a name.
4. Click "Save" to finish.

If you want to save a copy under a different name, use Save As (found under the "File" menu).

Why isn't my text showing up in Word?

If your text isn't showing up:

1. Check the font color: Ensure the font isn't set to white or the same color as the background.
2. Make sure you are in the editing mode: Verify that the document isn't in "Reading Mode" or "Print Preview," which might not allow text editing.
3. Scroll through the document: The text could be on another part of the page, especially if the margins are large or there's a page break.

If the issue persists, restarting Word or your computer could resolve any temporary glitches.

How do I change the font and size of my text?

To change the font and size:

1. Select the text you want to format.
2. Go to the Home tab on the ribbon.
3. In the Font group, select the desired font and size from the drop-down menus.

You can also adjust font size by using the increase or decrease font size buttons (two small A's with an up or down arrow) next to the font size box.

What is the difference between Save and Save As?

- Save: Saves changes to the current document without altering the original name or location.
- Save As: Allows you to create a copy of the document with a different name or file type. You can also change the location where the document is saved.

Use Save As if you need a different version or want to save in another format (e.g., PDF).

How do I change page margins in Word?

To change margins:

1. Go to the Layout tab on the ribbon.
2. In the Page Setup group, click on Margins.

3. Choose from the predefined margin options, or select Custom Margins to adjust the top, bottom, left, and right margins to your preferred size.

Adjusting margins is especially useful for ensuring your document meets specific formatting guidelines (e.g., for printing).

How do I insert a picture into my document?

To insert an image:

1. Go to the Insert tab on the ribbon.
2. Click on Pictures in the Illustrations group.
3. Choose whether to insert an image from your computer or online.
4. Select the image file and click Insert.

Once the picture is inserted, you can resize it and adjust the text wrapping to fit it into your document.

How do I fix an alignment issue in my document?

If your text is misaligned:

1. Select the text that needs alignment.
2. Go to the Home tab, in the Paragraph group.
3. Click on the appropriate alignment button:
   o   Align Left for left-aligned text.
   o   Center for centered text.
   o   Align Right for right-aligned text.
   o   Justify for text that stretches across the page evenly.

This ensures that your text is placed exactly where you want it.

How can I add page numbers to my document?

To add page numbers:

1. Go to the Insert tab.
2. In the Header & Footer group, click on Page Number.
3. Choose your preferred position (Top of Page, Bottom of Page) and format.

Once added, Word will automatically number the pages for you, which will update as the document changes.

How do I print my document?

To print your document:

1. Click on the File tab.
2. Select Print.
3. Choose your printer, number of copies, and print settings.
4. Click Print when you're ready.

Make sure to preview your document before printing to ensure everything is aligned correctly.

How do I undo or redo an action?

To undo an action:

1. Click the Undo button in the Quick Access Toolbar (or press Ctrl+Z).

To redo an action:

1. Click the Redo button in the Quick Access Toolbar (or press Ctrl+Y).

These options are lifesavers when you need to correct mistakes or return to a previous state.

How do I create a bulleted or numbered list?

To create a list:

1. Select the text you want to turn into a list.
2. Go to the Home tab.
3. In the Paragraph group, click on either the Bullets or Numbering button.

For more list customization, click the small drop-down arrow next to either button to select a different style or numbering format.

How do I change the document orientation (portrait or landscape)?

To change the orientation:

1. Go to the Layout tab.
2. Click Orientation in the Page Setup group.
3. Select either Portrait (vertical) or Landscape (horizontal).

This is useful when you need to switch the document format for wider content, like graphs or tables.

How do I enable or disable AutoCorrect?

To manage AutoCorrect settings:

1. Click on File, then Options.
2. In the Word Options window, click on Proofing.
3. Click on AutoCorrect Options.
4. Enable or disable specific AutoCorrect features as needed.

AutoCorrect helps you avoid typos by automatically fixing common mistakes as you type.

How do I track changes made to my document?

To track changes:

1. Go to the Review tab.
2. In the Tracking group, click on Track Changes.
3. Any edits made to the document will now be highlighted, and you'll be able to accept or reject them.

This is especially helpful when collaborating with others.

How do I add a hyperlink to my document?

To add a hyperlink:

1. Select the text you want to turn into a link.
2. Right-click and choose Link or press Ctrl+K.
3. In the dialog box, enter the URL or the path to the file you want to link to.
4. Click OK.

Hyperlinks are useful for adding external references or links to other sections of your document.

How do I recover a lost document?

If a document crashes or isn't saved:

1. Open Word again, and check for AutoRecover versions that might be available.
2. Go to File, then Info, and under Manage Document, look for Recover Unsaved Documents.
3. Select a recovered version and save it to your preferred location.

AutoSave and AutoRecover are lifesavers for unexpected situations.

How do I use a template in Word?

To use a template:

1. Click on File, then New.
2. Browse through the available templates, or search for one using the search bar.
3. Select the template you want, and it will open as a new document.

Templates are great for creating things like resumes, newsletters, or calendars quickly.

How do I insert a table into my document?

To insert a table:

1. Go to the Insert tab.
2. Click Table in the Tables group.
3. Choose the number of rows and columns you need, or click Insert Table for more customization.

Tables are excellent for organizing data in a clear, structured format.

How do I use the Review tab to add comments?

To add a comment:

1. Go to the Review tab.
2. In the Comments group, click on New Comment.
3. Type your comment in the sidebar.

This allows you to leave feedback or notes without altering the document content.

Summary

These FAQs should help clarify some of the most common beginner questions you may encounter as you explore Microsoft Word. With this newfound knowledge, you're now ready to continue using Word with more confidence, troubleshoot problems effectively

Index

www.ingramcontent.com/pod-product-compliance
Lightning Source LLC
LaVergne TN
LVHW051733050326
832903LV00023B/904